UNDER 125 CALORIES

UNDER 150 CALORIES

Better Homes and Gardens®

Low-Calorie DESSERTS

Each serving of flattering Peach-Orange Torte boasts a tender yellow cake on the bottom, a tangy peach-filled orange gelatin layer in the middle, and a generous dollop of low-calorie whipped topping on the top.

On the cover: *You'll welcome any one of these colorful low-calorie desserts—(in back, left to right) Tangy Lime Pie and Lemon-Berry Parfaits; (in middle) Choco-Mint Roll and Pineapple Cheesecake; and (in front) Berry-Rhubarb Shortcake and Cran-Tangerine Meringue.*

BETTER HOMES AND GARDENS BOOKS

Editorial Director: Don Dooley
Managing Editor: Malcolm E. Robinson   Art Director: John Berg
Food Editor: Nancy Morton
Senior Food Editor: Joyce Trollope
Associate Editors: Nancy Byal, Rosalie Riglin
Assistant Editors: Pat Olson, Sharyl Heiken, Elizabeth Strait, Sandra Mapes
Copy Editor: Lawrence Clayton
Designers: Julie Zesch, Harijs Priekulis

CONTENTS

EAT AND ENJOY DESSERTS

LOW-CALORIE DESSERTS FOR EVERYDAY

LOW-CALORIE DESSERTS FOR ENTERTAINING

LOW-CALORIE DESSERT SPECIALTIES

LOW-CALORIE DESSERTS IN MENUS

INDEX

Our seal assures you that every recipe in *Low-Calorie Desserts* is endorsed by the Better Homes and Gardens Test Kitchen. Each recipe has been thoroughly tested for family appeal, practicality, and deliciousness.

Eat and Enjoy Desserts

Does a desire for sweets lead you to stray from your diet? Are you a person who believes desserts only add 'empty' calories and cannot possibly be good for you? No matter which of the two categories you belong in, you can enjoy low-calorie desserts.

Whether you are on a regimented diet to lose weight or are simply 'cutting down' to maintain your present status, desserts *can* pose a problem. In fact, some seemingly determined people have given up on a weight-reducing plan simply because it did not include desserts. With the recipes in this book, you need not take such a drastic step.

Most nutritionists agree that a weight control program must meet your individual needs. Although for some people, the desire to eat sweets is small, for many others the urge is great. It is for these people that including an occasional low-calorie dessert in a weight-loss campaign aids the morale.

But how do you include desserts in a calorie-controlled plan? First, with the aid of your physician, design a nutritionally balanced diet. Then, as you plan menus, use a dessert to fulfill part of your nutritional needs. Select from this book's desserts, all of which have been trimmed of extra fats, sugars, and starches, and learn to stick faithfully to the specified servings. These are the only adjustments you need to make.

The most important consideration in weight control is to maintain a balanced diet. Once you have determined the number of calories

A well-rounded dinner

Chilled Eggnog Soufflé tops off a tempting low-calorie meal of roast chicken, broccoli spears, and apple-orange salad. (See page 86 for menu.)

What is a calorie?

A calorie is a measure of heat energy produced by food. In the laboratory, calories are measured in a calorimeter, an apparatus in which food is burned. A container that holds the food and oxygen is immersed in water, then the food inside is ignited by an electric fuse. As the food burns, one calorie is recorded for each degree the water temperature rises. In a similar manner, your body burns calories to provide energy. However, when you eat more food than the body can burn up as calories, the excess is converted to fat and a weight gain occurs.

---

you can consume and still lose weight, plan menus with a sensible approach to nutrition. The last section of the book (pages 84 to 92), which explains the Basic Four Food Groups along with low-calorie menu examples, helps you do this. In addition, this section shows you how to fit low-calorie desserts into calorie-controlled menus, and it has a complete Calorie Chart.

This book offers an appealing array of desserts that you can use in your menu plans to fulfill nutritive requirements. You will find low-calorie versions of favorites such as Bread Pudding and Baked Custard as well as exciting, new desserts such as Orange Alaskas and Apricot-Pineapple Kuchen. Specially developed recipes even make it possible for you to enjoy previously taboo desserts such as cakes, cookies, and pies. And for very limited diets, choose from the '60 calories and less' desserts set off by the 'under 60 calories' symbol.

low-calorie desserts
FOR EVERYDAY

Calorie-trimmed desserts no longer are limited just to dieters. The Orange Alaskas and Chilled Chocolate Dessert pictured here are two examples of the many inviting recipes in this section that the whole family will enjoy. In addition to the fruit, gelatin, pudding, and frozen desserts, make the special low-calorie cakes, cookies, pies, beverages, sauces, and toppings part of your daily menu repertoire.

Fruit Favorites

FRUIT WITH MELON ICE
103 calories/serving

Pictured on pages 84 and 85 —

1 large crenshaw or casaba melon
⅓ cup sugar
1 envelope unflavored gelatin
1 tablespoon lemon juice
1 medium pink grapefruit
2 medium oranges
1 medium banana
⅓ cup pomegranate seeds

Cut slice off bottom of melon. Using sawtooth cut, remove top third of melon. Remove seeds. Cut pulp from melon, reserving shell as serving bowl. Chill shell. Puree pulp (about 3 cups).

Combine sugar and gelatin; stir in 1 cup purée. Cook and stir till gelatin dissolves. Remove from heat; add remaining purée and lemon juice. Pour into a 4-cup freezer tray; freeze till firm. Break into chunks. Turn into chilled bowl; beat with electric mixer till smooth. Return to tray; freeze firm.

Peel and section grapefruit and oranges over bowl, catching juices. Slice banana; toss with fruit. Spoon fruit into 8 sherbets. Scoop ice into melon shell. Spoon ice over each serving. Garnish with pomegranate seeds. Serves 8.

MIXED FRUIT AMBROSIA
102 calories/serving

Drain one 11-ounce can mandarin oranges, reserving ½ cup syrup. In small saucepan blend reserved syrup, 2 teaspoons cornstarch, and 1 teaspoon honey. Cook and stir till thickened and bubbly. Reduce heat; cook and stir 1 minute. Remove from heat.

Stir in ¼ teaspoon vanilla. Cool 10 minutes without stirring. Stir in ⅓ cup yogurt. Stir in 1 medium banana, sliced; 1 cup fresh strawberries, halved; and 2 tablespoons shredded coconut, toasted. Chill. Makes 5 servings.

FRUIT AND CREAM COMPOTE
79 calories/serving

1 medium grapefruit
1 20-ounce can pineapple chunks (juice pack), drained
¾ cup fresh blueberries
½ cup cream-style cottage cheese
3 tablespoons skim milk
1 tablespoon sugar
¼ teaspoon rum flavoring
1 small banana, diced

Peel and section grapefruit over bowl. Stir in pineapple and berries; chill. Combine next 4 ingredients in blender container. Cover; blend smooth. Stir in banana; chill. Spoon fruit into compote. Pass sauce. Serves 8.

MINTED PINEAPPLE
87 calories/serving

1 20-ounce can pineapple chunks (juice pack)
1 tablespoon sugar
1 teaspoon cornstarch
4 fresh mint leaves or 6 drops mint extract
1 drop green food coloring
6 green maraschino cherries, quartered

Drain pineapple, reserving juice. In saucepan combine sugar and cornstarch; stir in reserved juice and mint. Cook and stir till thickened and bubbly. Tint green with food coloring. Stir in fruit. Chill several hours. Remove mint leaves before serving. Makes 5 servings.

Succulent fruit plus

Drape creamy banana-cottage cheese sauce over each serving of grapefruit, pineapple, and blueberries for inviting Fruit and Cream Compote.

APPLE FLUFF-TOPPED BERRIES
32 calories/serving

Just fold applesauce into whipped evaporated skim milk and serve over raspberries —

¼ **cup evaporated skim milk**
1 **tablespoon sugar**
1 **teaspoon lemon juice**
4 **drops red food coloring**
  Dash ground cinnamon
¼ **cup unsweetened applesauce**
2 **cups fresh red raspberries, chilled**

UNDER 60 CALORIES

Freeze evaporated milk till ice crystals form around edges. Add sugar, lemon juice, food coloring, and cinnamon; beat till stiff peaks form. Fold in applesauce. Chill, if desired. Divide berries among 8 serving dishes. Spoon topping over each serving. Makes 8 servings.

LEMON-BERRY PARFAITS
127 calories/serving

Pictured on the cover —

2 **egg yolks**
⅓ **cup sugar**
3 **tablespoons lemon juice**
2 **egg whites**
¼ **teaspoon cream of tartar**
2 **cups fresh strawberries, chilled**
2 **cups fresh blueberries, chilled**
½ **cup whipped low-calorie dessert topping**

Beat egg yolks and sugar till thick and lemon-colored. Add lemon juice. In saucepan cook and stir over medium-low heat till slightly thickened, about 6 to 8 minutes. Cool. Beat egg whites with cream of tartar till stiff peaks form. Fold yolk mixture into whites till well blended. Chill thoroughly.

Reserve 3 whole strawberries; quarter remaining strawberries. Arrange quartered strawberries in bottom of 6 parfait glasses; spoon *half* the lemon mixture over. Top with blueberries; spoon remaining lemon mixture over. Garnish with whipped topping and reserved strawberries, halved. Makes 6 servings.

PEARS IN CRANBERRY TAPIOCA
120 calories/serving

Apples are a good substitute for the pears —

1 **cup low-calorie cranberry juice cocktail**
¼ **cup jellied cranberry sauce**
2 **tablespoons quick-cooking tapioca**
½ **teaspoon ground ginger**
2 **fresh medium pears, peeled, cored, and coarsely cut up**

In saucepan combine first 4 ingredients. Let stand 5 minutes. Cook and stir over medium heat till thickened and bubbly. Stir in pears. Spoon into serving dishes; chill. Serves 4.

FRUIT SPARKLE CUP
54 calories/serving

UNDER 60 CALORIES

1 **cup honeydew melon balls**
1 **cup fresh dark sweet cherries, halved and pitted**
1 **cup seedless green grapes**
½ **teaspoon snipped candied ginger**
1 **cup low-calorie lemon-lime carbonated beverage, chilled**

Combine melon balls, cherries, grapes, and ginger; chill. At serving time, spoon into 5 sherbet dishes. Slowly pour carbonated beverage over each serving. Makes 5 servings.

LOW-CALORIE COOKING TIP

Make attractive melon pieces without adding calories. Scoop out perfectly round balls, using a long-handled melon baller.

Carbonated beverage adds an effervescent note to the fresh honeydew melon, dark sweet cherry, and green grape flavors in Fruit Sparkle Cup. To retain the most carbonation, pour the beverage slowly over the fruit.

GOLDEN PAPAYA DESSERT

107 calories/serving

The sauce made from custard mix (20 calories/ tablespoon) is delicious over other fresh fruit, too—

    1 fresh medium papaya
1½ cups reconstituted nonfat dry milk
    1 3-ounce package no-bake custard mix
 ½ teaspoon grated lemon peel
    1 tablespoon lemon juice
 ¼ cup unsweetened pineapple juice

Peel papaya; remove seeds and dice fruit (should have about 1½ cups). Using the 1½ cups reconstituted nonfat dry milk, prepare custard mix according to package directions. Cool to room temperature, stirring often. Stir in lemon peel and fruit juices.

Divide diced papaya among 6 serving dishes. Pour custard mixture over papaya. Chill desserts thoroughly. Makes 6 servings.

PEARS GERMAINE

102 calories/serving

    8 3x1½x¼-inch slices pound cake
 ⅓ cup low-calorie raspberry jam
    2 tablespoons water
    3 fresh medium pears
      Ascorbic acid color keeper or lemon
      juice mixed with water
    1 cup whipped low-calorie dessert
      topping
    1 teaspoon brandy flavoring

Line bottom of 8x8x2-inch baking dish with pound cake slices, cutting cake to fit the pan. Combine raspberry jam and water. Spread raspberry jam mixture over pound cake.

Peel, core, and slice pears. To keep fruit bright, dip in color keeper. Arrange pear slices over jam. Combine whipped topping and brandy flavoring; spread over pears. Cover; chill several hours. Serves 8.

FRUITS AU TANGERINE
91 calories/serving

Peach and plum slices are served in a golden, fresh-flavored tangerine sauce—

> 1 teaspoon unflavored gelatin
> 2 tablespoons sugar
> ¾ cup cold water
> ½ of 6-ounce can frozen tangerine juice
>   concentrate (⅓ cup)
>   • • •
> 1 tablespoon dry sherry
> 4 fresh medium peaches
> 4 fresh medium red plums

In small saucepan combine gelatin and sugar; stir in cold water. Stir over low heat till gelatin and sugar dissolve; stir in frozen juice concentrate and dry sherry. Chill till gelatin mixture is thickened.

At serving time, peel, pit, and slice peaches. Slice and pit plums. Combine peaches and plums; spoon fruit mixture evenly into 6 serving dishes. Beat thickened gelatin with rotary beater till smooth; pour over fruits in serving dishes. Makes 6 servings.

RASPBERRY-SAUCED KABOBS
121 calories/serving

Raspberry jam and lime juice make up the basting sauce for easy kabobed fruit and cake—

> 1 cup cubed fresh pineapple
> 1 cup fresh whole strawberries
> 1 firm medium banana, thickly sliced
>   (6 slices)
> 12 1-inch cubes pound cake
> ⅓ cup low-calorie raspberry jam
> 1 tablespoon lime juice
> 2 tablespoons water

On six 8-inch skewers, alternately thread cubed pineapple, strawberries, sliced banana, and pound cake. Combine raspberry jam, lime juice, and water. Baste fruit and cake with some of jam mixture. Grill over *hot* coals, turning often and basting occasionally, till heated through, 4 or 5 minutes. Makes 6 servings.

MINTED MELON CUP
57 calories/serving

> ¾ cup cold water
> 2 tablespoons frozen limeade
>   concentrate, thawed
> 4 drops mint extract
> 4 cups cantaloupe balls

Combine water, limeade concentrate, and mint extract. Pour over cantaloupe balls in deep bowl. Cover and chill several hours; stir once or twice. Serve in sherbets; garnish each serving with a sprig of mint, if desired. Serves 6.

CHILLED STRAWBERRY WHIP
50 calories/serving

Ready to serve in minutes—

> 1 cup fresh strawberries
> 3 egg whites
> ½ teaspoon vanilla
> ¼ cup sugar
>   Few drops red food coloring

Mash strawberries. Beat egg whites and vanilla till soft peaks form. Gradually add sugar, beating till stiff peaks form. Fold in mashed berries; stir in food coloring. Spoon into 6 sherbets; serve at once. Makes 6 servings.

BAKED APPLES WITH CHEESE
121 calories/serving

> 6 small baking apples, cored
> ¼ cup raisins
> 2 tablespoons sugar
> ½ teaspoon vanilla
> ½ cup yogurt
> ¼ cup shredded process American cheese

Peel strip from top of apples. Place in baking dish. In center of each, spoon in raisins. Combine 1 cup water, sugar, and vanilla. Pour syrup over apples; bake, uncovered, at 350° for 1 hour, basting occasionally with syrup. Combine yogurt and cheese. To serve, spoon cheese topping over each apple. Serves 6.

**Fruit is low
in calories**

Fresh fruit, naturally low in calories, is an excellent dessert idea. Specially packed canned fruits reduce calories for you, also. Choose from a variety of packs: juice pack, water pack, artificially sweetened, and calories reduced (slightly sweetened). Although regular syrup-pack fruits absorb sugar from the syrup, you can reduce some of the calories by rinsing the fruit with water before using.

CURRIED FRUIT COMPOTE

107 calories/serving

    1 16-ounce can peach slices (water pack)
    1 20-ounce can pitted tart red cherries,
       drained
    ½ cup raisins
    ¼ cup dark corn syrup
    1 teaspoon curry powder

Drain peaches, reserving liquid. Combine peaches, cherries, and raisins in a 1-quart casserole. Combine reserved liquid, corn syrup, and curry powder; stir into fruits. Bake, uncovered, at 350° for 30 minutes, stirring once or twice. Serve warm. Makes 8 servings.

GRAPEFRUIT AMBROSIA

109 calories/serving

    2 medium grapefruit, halved
    2 tablespoons brown sugar
    ¼ cup shredded coconut
    1 teaspoon rum flavoring

With knife, cut around fruit sections to loosen. Combine remaining ingredients. Sprinkle over fruit. Place in shallow baking pan. Bake at 400° for 20 minutes. Serves 4.

ROSY FRUIT COMPOTE

119 calories/serving

Cherries, peaches, and grapefruit bake in a spicy sauce—like a cobbler without the topping—

    1 20-ounce can pitted tart red cherries
    ¼ cup sugar
    1 tablespoon cornstarch
    ¼ teaspoon ground cinnamon
    ¼ teaspoon ground ginger
    6 drops red food coloring
    4 fresh medium peaches, peeled, pitted,
       and quartered
    1 medium grapefruit, peeled and
       sectioned

Drain cherries, reserving juice. In saucepan combine sugar, cornstarch, ground cinnamon, and ground ginger. Stir in cherry juice and food coloring. Cook and stir till mixture is thickened and bubbly. Stir in cherries.
   Place peach quarters and grapefruit sections in 10x6x1¾-inch baking dish. Pour cherry mixture over fruit. Cover and bake at 350° till fruit is tender and hot, about 40 minutes. Serve warm. Makes 6 servings.

Spoon an American cheese and yogurt topping over steaming, fresh-from-the-oven apples to make Baked Apples with Cheese. Serve with the basting syrup.

BITTER ORANGES
106 calories/serving

Honey adds sweetness to the tang—

1 cup water
½ cup unsweetened pineapple juice
1 tablespoon honey
• • •
4 medium navel oranges, peeled and
   sliced
¼ teaspoon grated orange peel

In medium saucepan combine water, pineapple juice, and honey. Bring to boiling; simmer 10 minutes. Cut orange slices in half; add to syrup. Bring to boiling again; simmer till oranges are heated through but still firm, 1 minute. Remove from heat. Stir in peel. Chill thoroughly. Serve cold. Makes 4 servings.

CHEESY BAKED APPLES
103 calories/serving

4 medium baking apples, peeled, cored,
   and cut in eighths
¼ cup water
2 teaspoons lemon juice
• • •
2 tablespoons sugar
1 tablespoon all-purpose flour
¼ teaspoon ground cinnamon
⅛ teaspoon salt
2 ounces process American cheese,
   shredded (½ cup)

Arrange apple slices in shallow baking dish; sprinkle with water and lemon juice. Mix sugar, flour, ground cinnamon, and salt; sprinkle over apples. Bake, covered, at 350° till apples are tender, about 45 minutes. Uncover; top with shredded cheese. Return to oven till cheese melts, 5 minutes. Serves 6.

Hot fruit duo
Fragrant, piping-hot fruit desserts such as bubbly Cheesy Baked Apples and Cranberry-Peach Cobbler are what make fruit desserts doubly popular.

CRANBERRY-PEACH COBBLER
111 calories/serving

½ cup sifted all-purpose flour
2 teaspoons sugar
1½ teaspoons baking powder
¼ teaspoon salt
¼ cup quick-cooking rolled oats
¼ cup reconstituted nonfat dry milk
1 beaten egg
1 teaspoon butter or margarine, melted
1 tablespoon cornstarch
¼ cup sugar
1 cup low-calorie cranberry juice
   cocktail
2 cups sliced, peeled fresh peaches
½ cup fresh cranberries

For topper, sift together flour, 2 teaspoons sugar, baking powder, and salt. Stir in oats. Blend milk, egg, and butter. Make well in dry ingredients; add liquid to flour mixture, stirring just to moisten. Set aside.

In saucepan combine cornstarch, ¼ cup sugar, and cranberry juice; cook and stir till thick and bubbly. Stir in peaches and cranberries. Cook, uncovered, till cranberry skins pop, about 5 minutes. Pour into 8¼x1¾-inch round ovenware cake dish. Immediately spoon on topper in 8 mounds. Bake at 400° for 20 to 25 minutes. Serve warm. Makes 8 servings.

RHUBARB CRUNCH
104 calories/serving

⅓ cup sugar
2 teaspoons cornstarch
1 pound fresh rhubarb, diced (4 cups)
2 tablespoons orange juice
½ cup packaged biscuit mix
1 tablespoon sugar
¼ teaspoon grated orange peel
1 tablespoon skim milk

Combine first 2 ingredients; stir in rhubarb and orange juice. Turn into 8x8x2-inch baking pan. Combine biscuit mix, 1 tablespoon sugar, and peel. Slowly add milk, mixing lightly with a fork. Sprinkle over rhubarb. Bake at 350° for 40 to 45 minutes. Serves 8.

16

Tempting
Gelatin Desserts

CHILLED EGGNOG SOUFFLÉ
91 calories/serving

Pictured on page 4 —

   1 envelope unflavored gelatin
   ½ cup nonfat dry milk powder
   ⅓ cup sugar
   ¼ teaspoon salt
   4 beaten egg yolks
   1 teaspoon rum flavoring
   4 egg whites
     Ground nutmeg

In saucepan combine first 4 ingredients; stir in 1½ cups cold water. Blend in yolks. Stir over low heat till mixture just coats metal spoon. Remove from heat; stir in flavoring. Chill till partially set; stir occasionally. Beat whites to stiff peaks; fold into gelatin. Turn into a 4-cup soufflé dish with foil collar; top with nutmeg. Chill till firm. Serves 8.

HONEYDEW-LIME MOLD
64 calories/serving

In saucepan mix 1 envelope unflavored gelatin and ¼ cup sugar. Add ½ cup cold water; stir over low heat till gelatin dissolves. Stir in ¼ cup low-calorie lemon-lime carbonated beverage, ¼ cup lime juice, 3 or 4 drops green food coloring, and 1 drop peppermint extract. Add ¼ cup evaporated skim milk to ⅓ cup gelatin mixture. (Mixture may look curdled.) Chill till partially set; whip till fluffy. Pour into a 4½-cup mold. Chill till *almost* firm.

   Combine ¾ cup low-calorie lemon-lime carbonated beverage with remaining gelatin; chill till partially set. Fold in 1 cup honeydew melon balls. Pour over whipped layer. Chill till firm. Garnish with fresh mint. Serves 6.

PINEAPPLE CHEESECAKE
78 calories/serving

Pictured on the cover —

   1 cup evaporated skim milk
   1 20-ounce can crushed pineapple
     (juice pack)
   2 envelopes unflavored gelatin
   2 cups dry cottage cheese
   2 egg yolks
   2 tablespoons lemon juice
   ¼ teaspoon yellow food coloring
   2 egg whites
   ¼ cup sugar
   1 8-ounce can pineapple slices
     (juice pack), drained
   2 tablespoons graham cracker crumbs

Chill evaporated milk in freezer till icy cold. Drain crushed pineapple, reserving juice. In saucepan soften gelatin in reserved juice. Stir over low heat till gelatin dissolves. Cool. Place gelatin mixture, cheese, yolks, lemon juice, food coloring, and *half* the crushed pineapple in blender container; blend smooth. Stir in remaining crushed fruit.

   Beat egg whites to soft peaks; gradually add sugar, beating to stiff peaks. In large bowl whip icy milk to soft peaks. Fold in pineapple mixture and egg whites. Pour into 10-inch springform pan. Chill; remove sides of pan. Top with pineapple slices, cracker crumbs, and fresh mint, if desired. Serves 16.

Fresh as spring

A hint of peppermint lingers after you taste Honeydew-Lime Mold. Cool and inviting melon balls and lemon-lime beverage come together in this finale. →

LEMON-COCONUT SQUARES
66 calories/serving

  1 envelope unflavored gelatin
¼ cup sugar
¼ teaspoon grated lemon peel
¼ cup lemon juice
  1 envelope from a 2½-ounce package
     low-calorie dessert topping mix
¼ teaspoon yellow food coloring
  3 tablespoons flaked coconut, toasted

In saucepan combine gelatin and sugar; add 1 cup cold water. Stir over low heat till gelatin dissolves. Add ½ cup cold water, peel, and juice. Chill till partially set. Prepare topping mix following package directions. Tint with food coloring. Fold in gelatin. Turn into 8x8x2-inch baking dish. Chill till firm. Cut in squares. Top with coconut. Serves 9.

Ground nutmeg decorates the top and flavors the zwieback crumb crust of Snowy Vanilla Torte, a light, yet unbelievably rich-flavored gelatin dessert.

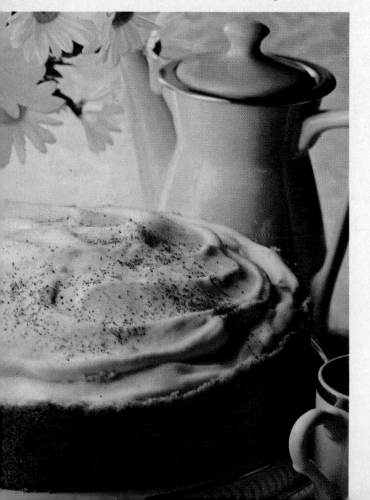

CINNAMON-PEAR MOLD
62 calories/serving

  1 16-ounce can pear halves (water pack)
¼ cup sugar
  1 tablespoon vinegar
  6 whole cloves
  6 inches stick cinnamon
  1 4-serving envelope low-calorie
     cherry-flavored gelatin

Drain pears, reserving liquid. Add water to make ¾ cup. Cut up pears. Combine liquid, sugar, vinegar, and spices; bring to boil. Add pears. Simmer, covered, 10 minutes. Strain pears, reserving hot liquid. Dissolve gelatin in hot liquid; stir in 1 cup cold water. Chill till partially set. Remove spices from fruit; fold fruit into gelatin. Pour into 3½-cup mold. Chill till firm. Makes 6 servings.

SNOWY VANILLA TORTE
134 calories/serving

12 zwieback, finely crushed
  2 tablespoons butter, melted
¼ teaspoon ground nutmeg
½ cup sifted powdered sugar
  1 envelope unflavored gelatin
  2 egg whites
¼ teaspoon grated lemon peel
  1 tablespoon lemon juice
½ teaspoon vanilla
  1 envelope from a 2½-ounce package
     low-calorie dessert topping mix
  1 cup low-calorie imitation sour cream
     or 1 cup yogurt mixed with 2
     teaspoons granulated sugar

Combine first 3 ingredients. Press on bottom and sides of a 7-inch springform pan; chill. Combine sugar, gelatin, and dash salt; stir in 1¼ cups cold water. Stir over medium heat till gelatin dissolves. Chill till partially set. Add whites, peel, juice, and vanilla; beat till very fluffy. Chill till partially set.

  Prepare topping following package directions; fold into gelatin along with imitation sour cream. Pile into crust; dash with nutmeg, if desired. Chill till firm. Makes 12 servings.

CRAN-PINEAPPLE DESSERT
94 calories/serving

   1 6-ounce can evaporated skim milk
   1 20-ounce can pineapple chunks
      (water pack)
   1 envelope unflavored gelatin
   ½ cup sugar
   ½ teaspoon vanilla
   1 tablespoon lemon juice
   1 tablespoon cornstarch
   1¼ cups low-calorie cranberry
      juice cocktail

Chill milk in freezer till icy cold. Drain pineapple, reserving ¾ cup liquid. In saucepan mix gelatin, ¼ *cup* sugar, ¼ teaspoon salt, and liquid. Stir over low heat till gelatin and sugar dissolve; stir in vanilla. Chill till partially thickened. Beat till fluffy.

   Coarsely chop pineapple. Whip milk to soft peaks; combine with lemon juice and pineapple. Fold into gelatin. Pile into a 6½-cup mold. Chill till firm. Mix ¼ cup sugar and cornstarch; add cranberry cocktail. Cook and stir till thickened; cook 2 minutes more. Chill. Serve sauce with unmolded gelatin. Serves 10.

BERRY-SAUCED ORANGE MOLD
88 calories/serving

   1 3-ounce package regular orange-
      flavored gelatin
   ¼ teaspoon grated orange peel
   ½ cup orange juice
   1 egg white
   1 10-ounce package frozen raspberries,
      thawed
   2 teaspoons cornstarch

In large bowl dissolve gelatin in 1 cup boiling water. Stir in peel, juice, and ¼ cup cold water. Chill till partially set. Add egg white. Beat with electric mixer till fluffy. Pour into eight ½-cup molds. Chill till firm.

   Drain berries, reserving syrup. Blend cornstarch and syrup. Cook and stir over medium heat till thickened and bubbly; cook 1 minute more. Remove from heat; stir in berries. Chill. Serve sauce with unmolded gelatin. Serves 8.

CHERRY-RICE BAVARIAN
108 calories/serving

   1 16-ounce can dark sweet cherries
      (artificially sweetened)
   ⅓ cup sugar
   1 envelope unflavored gelatin
   1 cup low-calorie lemon-lime
      carbonated beverage
   1 tablespoon lemon juice
   ½ cup uncooked long grain rice, cooked
   1 envelope from a 2½-ounce package
      low-calorie dessert topping mix

Drain cherries, reserving ½ cup liquid. Halve and pit cherries. In saucepan combine sugar, gelatin, dash salt, and reserved liquid. Stir over low heat till gelatin dissolves; cool. Stir in carbonated beverage, lemon juice, and rice. Chill till partially set. Prepare topping mix following package directions. Fold topping and cherries into gelatin mixture. Pour into a 5½-cup mold. Makes 10 servings.

GRAPE SNOW WITH CUSTARD
68 calories/serving

   1 envelope unflavored gelatin
   ¼ cup sugar
   ½ of 6-ounce can frozen grape juice
      concentrate (⅓ cup)
   2 egg whites
   ¾ cup reconstituted nonfat dry milk
   2 beaten egg yolks
   1 tablespoon sugar

In saucepan combine gelatin, ¼ cup sugar, dash salt, and 1½ cups cold water. Stir over low heat till gelatin and sugar dissolve. Remove from heat. Stir in juice concentrate till thawed. Chill till partially set. Turn into large bowl; add egg whites. Beat with electric mixer till light and fluffy. Pour into a 6½-cup mold. Chill till firm.

   In saucepan combine milk, egg yolks, 1 tablespoon sugar, and dash salt. Cook and stir over low heat till mixture coats metal spoon. Remove from heat. Place in pan of cold water; stir a few minutes. Chill. Serve sauce with unmolded gelatin. Serves 10.

ROSY APPLESAUCE FLUFF

44 calories/serving

A blushing pink dessert—

1 4-serving envelope low-calorie
   raspberry-flavored gelatin
1¼ cups boiling water
1 8-ounce can applesauce (water pack)
2 tablespoons lemon juice
2 egg whites
  Dash salt
2 tablespoons sugar

Dissolve raspberry-flavored gelatin in 1¼ cups boiling water. Stir applesauce and lemon juice into gelatin. Chill till partially set.

Beat egg whites with salt till soft peaks form. Gradually add sugar, beating till stiff peaks form. Fold beaten egg whites into gelatin mixture. Mound in sherbet dishes; chill till firm. Makes 6 servings.

Use a little bottled cocktail mix to prepare refreshing Mai Tai Banana Mold. Fresh banana slices and pineapple juice are part of the creamy dessert mold.

MAI TAI BANANA MOLD

119 calories/serving

¼ cup sugar
1 envelope unflavored gelatin
2 beaten egg yolks
½ cup unsweetened pineapple juice
½ cup bottled nonalcoholic mai tai
   cocktail mix
2 egg whites
¼ teaspoon cream of tartar
1 envelope from a 2½-ounce package
   low-calorie dessert topping mix
2 medium bananas, sliced
  Ascorbic acid color keeper or lemon
   juice mixed with water

In saucepan combine sugar, gelatin, and dash salt. Stir in yolks; blend in pineapple juice. Cook and stir till mixture thickens. Stir in mai tai mix. Chill till partially set. Beat whites with cream of tartar to stiff peaks; fold into gelatin. Prepare topping mix following package directions; fold into gelatin. Reserve a few banana slices in color keeper for garnish. Fold in remaining fruit; turn into 4½-cup mold. Chill till firm. Makes 8 servings.

CREAMY RASPBERRY SWIRL

116 calories/serving

2 envelopes unflavored gelatin
1 10-ounce package frozen raspberries,
   thawed
1 6-ounce can frozen Hawaiian punch
   concentrate
1 cup low-calorie imitation sour cream
   or 1 cup yogurt mixed with 2
   teaspoons sugar

In saucepan soften gelatin in ½ cup cold water; stir over low heat till dissolved. Drain berries, reserving juice. Stir juice, punch concentrate, and 1¾ cups water into gelatin. Slowly blend *1 cup* gelatin mixture into imitation sour cream. Chill both mixtures till partially set. Fold berries into plain mixture. Layer fruit-filled and creamy mixtures in 5½-cup mold. Cut through with spatula to marble. Chill till firm. Makes 9 servings.

MAPLE DESSERT CUPS

44 calories/serving

Equally good chilled or frozen—

- **1 envelope unflavored gelatin**
- **2 tablespoons brown sugar**
- **1 6-ounce can evaporated skim milk (⅔ cup)**
- **1 teaspoon maple flavoring**
- **1 egg white**
- **1 tablespoon brown sugar**
- **1 tablespoon grape nuts cereal**

In saucepan combine gelatin and 2 tablespoons brown sugar; stir in ½ cup cold water. Stir over medium heat till gelatin and sugar dissolve. Remove from heat; stir in evaporated skim milk and maple flavoring. Pour mixture into large bowl; chill till partially thickened.

Beat egg white with remaining brown sugar till stiff peaks form. Beat chilled gelatin mixture with electric mixer till light and fluffy. Fold in whipped egg white. Spoon into 8 paper bake cups in muffin pans. Sprinkle grape nuts cereal atop each. Chill till firm or freeze. Makes 8 servings.

ORANGE-PUMPKIN FLUFF

86 calories/serving

Whip gelatin and egg whites in one step—

- **1 3-ounce package regular orange-flavored gelatin**
- **1 cup canned pumpkin**
- **¼ teaspoon grated orange peel**
- **¼ teaspoon pumpkin pie spice**
- **2 egg whites**
- **2 tablespoons sugar**

In small bowl dissolve gelatin in 1 cup boiling water. Stir in pumpkin, orange peel, and pumpkin pie spice. Chill till partially set.

Add unbeaten egg whites and sugar to gelatin mixture. Beat with electric mixer till mixture is light-colored and fluffy, about 6 to 10 minutes. Chill till mixture mounds when spooned. Spoon gelatin into 6 sherbet dishes; chill till firm. Makes 6 servings.

Combine fresh rhubarb and low-calorie strawberry-flavored gelatin for the dessert-winning flavor combination found in Strawberry-Rhubarb Whip.

STRAWBERRY-RHUBARB WHIP

51 calories/serving

Fold in beaten egg whites for better volume—

- **3 cups fresh rhubarb, cut in 1-inch slices**
- **¼ cup sugar**
- **1 4-serving envelope low-calorie strawberry-flavored gelatin**
- **2 egg whites**

In saucepan combine rhubarb, sugar, and ¼ cup water. Bring to boiling, stirring occasionally. Cover and cook over medium heat for 8 to 10 minutes, stirring often. Add gelatin; continue to cook and stir till gelatin dissolves. Stir in ½ cup cold water. Chill gelatin mixture till partially set.

With electric mixer or rotary beater, whip gelatin mixture till light and fluffy. Beat egg whites till stiff peaks form; fold into gelatin mixture. Spoon into sherbet dishes; chill till serving time. Garnish with fresh strawberry halves, if desired. Makes 6 servings.

Compare calorie counts of gelatin

When making gelatin-based desserts, reduce the calorie count considerably by using either an unflavored or a low-calorie fruit-flavored gelatin. These gelatins contain only about 34 calories per envelope compared to around 315 calories per package for the regular fruit-flavored gelatins. You save 281 calories.

FRUIT FLUFF PARFAITS
82 calories/serving

A pleasing blend of pineapple and rhubarb—

    1 8½-ounce can pineapple tidbits
        (juice pack)
    2 cups fresh rhubarb, cut in
        1-inch pieces
    ¼ cup sugar
        Dash salt
    6 drops red food coloring
            • • •
    1 4-serving envelope low-calorie
        raspberry-flavored gelatin
    ⅓ cup nonfat dry milk powder

Drain pineapple tidbits, reserving ⅓ *cup* of the juice. In saucepan combine reserved juice with rhubarb, sugar, and salt. Cook, covered, over medium heat for 8 to 10 minutes, stirring often. Add pineapple tidbits and red food coloring; cool thoroughly.

Dissolve raspberry-flavored gelatin in 1 cup boiling water; add ½ cup cold water. Cool gelatin to room temperature; stir in nonfat dry milk powder. Chill till gelatin is partially set. Fold *half* the gelatin mixture into *half* the rhubarb mixture; spoon into parfait glasses. Beat remaining gelatin with electric mixer till soft peaks form; fold into remaining rhubarb mixture. Spoon into parfait glasses atop unwhipped layer. Chill. Makes 6 servings.

ANGEL-LIME DESSERT
125 calories/serving

Grapefruit juice adds tang—

Dissolve one 3-ounce package *regular* lime-flavored gelatin in 1½ cups boiling water; stir in ½ cup unsweetened grapefruit juice. Chill till partially set. Using ½ cup reconstituted nonfat dry milk, prepare one 2-ounce package *regular* dessert topping mix following package directions. Fold gelatin and 3 cups angel cake cubes into topping. Turn into 10x6x1¾-inch dish. Chill till firm. Makes 10 servings.

STRAWBERRY CHARLOTTE RUSSE
91 calories/serving

    ¼ cup evaporated skim milk
    1 4-serving envelope low-calorie
        strawberry-flavored gelatin
    1 cup fresh strawberries, sliced
    2 tablespoons sugar
    2 egg whites
    2 tablespoons lemon juice
   16 ladyfingers, split lengthwise
    2 tablespoons low-calorie strawberry
        preserves

In shallow container chill evaporated milk in freezer till icy cold. In large bowl dissolve gelatin in ½ cup boiling water; stir in ½ cup cold water. Stir in strawberries, sugar, egg whites, and lemon juice. Cool thoroughly.

Meanwhile, place 16 ladyfinger halves together with strawberry preserves to form 8 sandwiches; arrange 4 sandwiches lengthwise on bottom of waxed paper-lined 9x5x3-inch loaf pan. Set aside the remaining 4 sandwiches. Stand remaining 16 ladyfinger halves around sides of pan, trimming to fit, if necessary.

Whip gelatin till light. Whip icy cold milk till soft peaks form; fold into gelatin mixture. Chill till mixture mounds. Carefully turn *half* the gelatin mixture into ladyfinger-lined pan. Place remaining 4 ladyfinger sandwiches lengthwise atop; cover with remaining gelatin. Chill till firm. Remove from pan; remove waxed paper. Garnish with halved strawberries, if desired. Makes 12 servings.

SPICED PEACH DESSERT
121 calories/serving

1 16-ounce can peach halves (water
   pack)
⅓ cup sugar
1 tablespoon vinegar
8 whole cloves
6 inches stick cinnamon
1 4-serving-envelope low-calorie
   lemon-flavored gelatin
1 3-ounce package Neufchâtel cheese
1 tablespoon skim milk
1 tablespoon finely chopped walnuts

Drain peaches, reserving liquid. Add water to liquid, if necessary, to make ¾ cup. In saucepan combine reserved liquid, sugar, vinegar, cloves, and cinnamon; bring to boil. Add peaches; simmer, covered, 10 minutes. Strain peaches, reserving hot syrup. Discard spices. Dissolve gelatin in hot peach syrup; stir in 1 cup cold water. Chill till partially set.

Meanwhile, whip Neufchâtel cheese with milk till fluffy; stir in finely chopped walnuts. Fill peach cavities with cheese. Place filled peach halves in 6 sherbets. Gently spoon gelatin over peaches and Neufchâtel cheese. Chill till firm. Makes 6 servings.

Treat strawberry lovers to triple berry-flavored Strawberry Charlotte Russe. Spongy ladyfingers sandwiched with strawberry preserves are layered in the fluffy strawberry gelatin that is garnished with fresh berries.

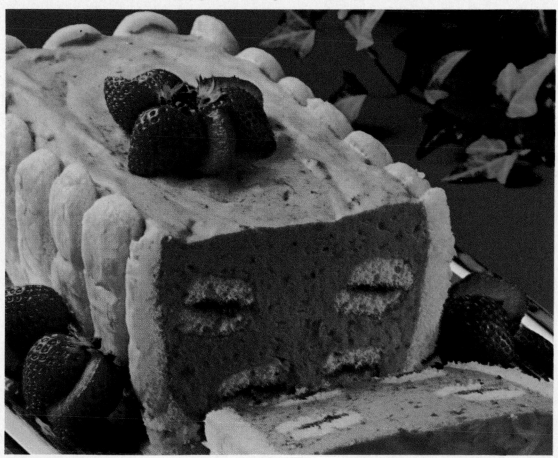

Plain and Fancy Puddings

AMBROSIA CREAM PUFFS
132 calories/serving

    ½ cup orange juice
    1 tablespoon cornstarch
    1 cup yogurt
    1 medium banana, finely chopped
    1 egg white
    2 tablespoons sugar
      Cream Puffs
    2 tablespoons shredded coconut, toasted

In saucepan blend orange juice and cornstarch. Cook and stir till thickened and bubbly. Remove from heat; cool slightly. Fold in yogurt and banana. Chill. Beat egg white with sugar to stiff peaks. Fold into yogurt mixture. Spoon into Cream Puffs. Garnish with toasted coconut. Put tops on puffs. Serves 8.

CREAM PUFFS
70 calories/cream puff

    2 tablespoons butter or margarine
    ½ cup boiling water
    ½ cup sifted all-purpose flour
    ⅛ teaspoon salt
    2 eggs

In saucepan melt butter in boiling water. Add flour and salt all at once; stir vigorously. Cook and stir till mixture forms a ball that doesn't separate. Remove from heat; cool slightly. Add eggs, one at a time, beating well after each addition till smooth.

Drop by heaping tablespoons, 3 inches apart, on lightly greased baking sheet. Bake at 450° for 15 minutes. Reduce heat to 325°; bake 10 minutes. Remove from oven; cut off tops. Turn oven off; return cream puffs to oven to dry, 20 minutes. Cool on rack. Makes 8.

CHILLED CHOCOLATE DESSERT
92 calories/serving

Pictured on pages 6 and 7 —

In saucepan mix ⅔ cup nonfat dry milk powder, ⅓ cup sugar, 2 tablespoons cornstarch, 2 tablespoons unsweetened cocoa powder, 1 envelope unflavored gelatin, and ⅛ teaspoon salt. Stir in 1½ cups cold water. Cook and stir till thickened and bubbly. Stir moderate amount of hot mixture into 3 beaten egg yolks; return to hot mixture. Cook and stir 1 minute more. Cool till partially thickened.

Beat 3 egg whites with 1 teaspoon vanilla and ¼ teaspoon cream of tartar till stiff peaks form. Fold into chocolate mixture. Fold in 1 cup *whipped* low-calorie dessert topping. Spoon chocolate mixture into a 5½-cup mold. Chill till firm. Makes 10 servings.

PEACH PUDDING
45 calories/serving

UNDER 60 CALORIES

Puree one 8-ounce can peaches (juice pack), chilled and drained, with 2 teaspoons lemon juice; stir in few drops almond extract. In large bowl, beat 2 egg whites with ¼ teaspoon cream of tartar to soft peaks. Gradually add 2 tablespoons powdered sugar, beating to stiff peaks. Fold peach purée into egg white mixture. Pile into 4 sherbet dishes. Serve at once. Makes 4 servings.

Matchless cream puffs

Orange juice, yogurt, and banana produce the →
tangy fruit flavor for the Ambrosia Cream Puffs fill-
ing. Toasted coconut decorates the top of the filling.

BANANA BREAD PUDDING
138 calories/serving

  1½ cups apricot nectar
  2 beaten egg yolks
  ¼ cup sugar
  1 medium banana, sliced
  3 slices day-old bread, cut in
      ½-inch cubes
  2 egg whites
  ½ teaspoon vanilla
  ¼ teaspoon cream of tartar

Combine nectar, egg yolks, *2 tablespoons* sugar, and banana; stir in bread. Spoon into 1-quart casserole. Bake at 350° for 25 minutes. Beat egg whites, vanilla, and cream of tartar to soft peaks. Gradually add remaining sugar, beating to stiff peaks. Spread meringue over hot pudding, sealing to edge. Bake 12 to 15 minutes more. Makes 6 servings.

Bread pudding takes on a delightful new look and taste. For Banana Bread Pudding, a light meringue topping covers a flavorful fruit filling.

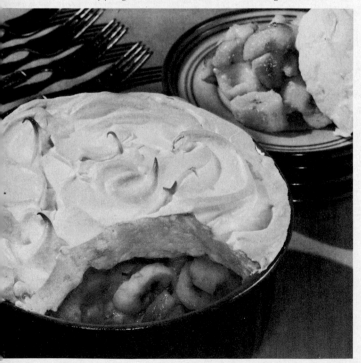

VANILLA PUDDING
123 calories/serving with sugar
 75 calories/serving with noncaloric sweetener

  ¼ cup sugar or noncaloric sweetener to
      equal ¼ cup sugar
  ⅔ cup nonfat dry milk powder
  2 tablespoons cornstarch
  1 well-beaten egg
  1 teaspoon vanilla

In saucepan blend first 3 ingredients and dash salt; stir in 1½ cups water. Cook and stir over medium heat till thickened and bubbly. Cook and stir 2 minutes. Remove from heat.
  Stir moderate amount of hot mixture into egg; return to hot mixture. Cook and stir 2 minutes more. Remove from heat; add vanilla. Pour into serving dishes; chill. Serves 4.

CHOCOLATE PUDDING
139 calories/serving with sugar
 91 calories/serving with noncaloric sweetener

Follow directions for Vanilla Pudding, adding 3 tablespoons unsweetened cocoa powder to sugar, milk, cornstarch, and salt. Serves 4.

FLUFFY TAPIOCA PUDDING
98 calories/serving with sugar
65 calories/serving with noncaloric sweetener

  ⅔ cup nonfat dry milk powder
  2 tablespoons quick-cooking tapioca
  ¼ cup sugar or noncaloric sweetener to
      equal ¼ cup sugar
  2 beaten egg yolks
  ½ teaspoon vanilla
  2 egg whites

In saucepan dissolve dry milk in 1½ cups water; stir in tapioca, sugar or noncaloric sweetener, and ¼ teaspoon salt. Let stand 5 minutes. Stir in egg yolks; bring to boiling, stirring constantly. Remove from heat (mixture will be thin); stir in vanilla. Beat egg whites to stiff peaks. Gradually fold into hot mixture. Chill. Spoon into dishes; sprinkle with ground nutmeg, if desired. Serves 6.

Calorie-trimmed puddings

Lower the calories in puddings by using reconstituted nonfat dry milk (82 calories/cup) or skim milk (105 calories/cup) in place of whole milk (160 calories/cup).

BERRY-LEMON-RICE PUDDING
121 calories/serving

Another time, substitute strawberries or raspberries for the blueberries—

  1⅓ **cups water**
    1 **6-ounce can evaporated skim milk (⅔ cup)**
  ⅓ **cup uncooked long grain rice**
    1 **beaten egg yolk**
    2 **tablespoons sugar**
    2 **tablespoons lemon juice**
  ¼ **teaspoon salt**
    1 **teaspoon vanilla**
  ¼ **teaspoon grated lemon peel**
    3 **egg whites**
  ¼ **teaspoon cream of tartar**
    2 **tablespoons sugar**
  ¾ **cup fresh blueberries**

In medium saucepan combine water, evaporated milk, and rice. Bring to boiling. Reduce heat; cook, covered, over low heat for 20 minutes, stirring often. Uncover; cook 5 minutes more. Combine egg yolk, 2 tablespoons sugar, lemon juice, and salt. Stir moderate amount of hot mixture into yolk mixture; return to saucepan. Cook and stir over low heat till thickened slightly, 3 to 4 minutes. Remove from heat; stir in vanilla and lemon peel. Cool thoroughly.

Beat egg whites and cream of tartar till soft peaks form. Gradually add remaining 2 tablespoons sugar, beating until stiff peaks form. Fold egg whites into rice pudding. Fold in blueberries. Chill well. Makes 6 servings.

Add a refreshing and satisfying note to a summer dinner by piling light and fluffy Berry-Lemon-Rice Pudding into glistening stemmed sherbet glasses.

BAKED INDIAN PUDDING
126 calories/serving

Whipped topping garnishes each serving—

In 2-quart saucepan combine 1 cup nonfat dry milk powder, ⅓ cup yellow cornmeal, 2 tablespoons sugar, ⅛ teaspoon salt, and ⅛ teaspoon baking soda; stir in 1¼ cups water. Cook and stir till thick and bubbly. Remove from heat. Combine 1 well-beaten egg, 3 tablespoons dark molasses, ¼ teaspoon ground cinnamon, ⅛ teaspoon ground ginger, and 1 cup water; gradually stir into cornmeal mixture.

Pour into 1-quart casserole. Bake, uncovered, at 300° till knife inserted off-center comes out clean, about 1 hour and 20 minutes. Spoon pudding into serving dishes. Spoon 1 tablespoon *whipped* low-calorie dessert topping over each serving. Serves 6.

BAKED CUSTARD

89 calories/serving with sugar
66 calories/serving with noncaloric sweetener

Simply combine ingredients, then bake—

3 beaten eggs
3 tablespoons sugar or noncaloric
    sweetener to equal ¼ cup sugar
2 cups reconstituted nonfat dry milk,
    scalded and slightly cooled
½ teaspoon vanilla

Combine beaten eggs, sugar or noncaloric sweetener, and ¼ teaspoon salt. Slowly stir in slightly cooled milk and vanilla. Pour into six 5-ounce custard cups; set cups in shallow pan on oven rack. Pour hot water into pan 1 inch deep. Bake at 325° till knife inserted off-center comes out clean, 55 to 60 minutes. Serve warm or chilled. Makes 6 servings.

Add Peaches in Custard Creme to your list of favorite recipes. A ring of peaches nestled in bubbling, caramelized sugar crowns the spicy custard.

STIRRED CUSTARD

73 calories/serving

Good served alone or over fresh fruit—

2 beaten eggs
1 tablespoon sugar
    Dash salt
    Noncaloric sweetener to equal 2
        tablespoons sugar
2 cups reconstituted nonfat dry milk,
    scalded and slightly cooled
½ teaspoon vanilla

Combine all ingredients *except* vanilla. Cook slowly, stirring constantly, till mixture coats a metal spoon; remove from heat. (Mixture will be thin.) Cool at once by placing pan in cold water. Stir a few minutes. Add vanilla. Chill. Makes 5 servings.

PEACHES IN CUSTARD CREME

144 calories/serving

Contains a hint of nutmeg—

1 16-ounce can peach slices (juice pack)
3 beaten eggs
1 6-ounce can evaporated skim milk
    (⅔ cup)
1 tablespoon granulated sugar
¼ teaspoon ground nutmeg
½ teaspoon vanilla
3 tablespoons brown sugar

Reserve 10 small peach slices. Puree remaining peaches with juice in blender (makes about 1⅓ cups). In saucepan combine pureed peaches, milk, eggs, granulated sugar, nutmeg, and dash salt. Cook and stir over low heat till mixture coats a metal spoon, about 12 minutes. Cook 2 minutes more. Stir in vanilla. Immediately turn custard mixture into 3-cup soufflé dish. Chill thoroughly.

At serving time, sift brown sugar evenly over custard by pressing through sieve. Set in ovenproof dish of cracked ice and broil 3 to 4 inches from heat just till sugar caramelizes, 4 to 5 minutes. Watch carefully. Garnish with reserved peaches. Makes 5 servings.

BREAD PUDDING

123 calories/serving with sugar
80 calories/serving with noncaloric sweetener

An adaptation of an old favorite—

   2 **beaten eggs**
2¼ **cups reconstituted nonfat dry milk**
   1 **teaspoon vanilla**
  ½ **teaspoon ground cinnamon**
  ¼ **teaspoon salt**
   2 **slices day-old bread, cut in**
      1-inch cubes
  ⅓ **cup sugar or noncaloric sweetener**
      to equal ⅓ cup sugar

Combine eggs, milk, vanilla, cinnamon, and salt; stir in bread cubes. Stir in sugar or noncaloric sweetener. Pour mixture into 8¼x1¾-inch round ovenware cake dish. Place pan in larger shallow pan on oven rack; pour hot water into larger pan 1 inch deep. Bake at 350° till knife inserted off-center comes out clean, about 35 minutes. Makes 6 servings.

PINEAPPLE SPONGE

113 calories/serving

Fluffy custard with fruit flavor—

  1 **cup reconstituted nonfat dry milk**
  4 **beaten egg yolks**
  2 **tablespoons sugar**
  1 **20-ounce can crushed pineapple**
     (juice pack), drained
  1 **teaspoon vanilla**
     • • •
  4 **egg whites**
  2 **tablespoons sugar**

In heavy saucepan combine milk, egg yolks, and 2 tablespoons sugar; cook over low heat, stirring constantly, till mixture coats a metal spoon. Remove from heat; stir in pineapple and vanilla. Cool quickly by placing pan in cold water; stir a few minutes. Beat egg whites to soft peaks. Gradually add remaining sugar, beating to stiff peaks. Gently fold egg whites into cooled custard mixture. Spoon into serving dishes; chill. Makes 8 servings.

Test for the doneness of low-calorie baked custard mixtures just as you do for standard custard recipes. Insert a knife halfway between center and edge. When the knife comes out clean, it is done.

PEACHY FLOATING ISLAND

97 calories/serving

   2 **egg whites**
   1 **tablespoon sugar**
1¼ **cups reconstituted nonfat dry milk**
   1 **egg**
   2 **egg yolks**
   2 **tablespoons sugar**
    Dash salt
  ¾ **teaspoon vanilla**
   3 **fresh medium peaches, peeled, pitted,**
     and sliced

Beat egg whites till soft peaks form. Gradually add 1 tablespoon sugar, beating to stiff peaks. In skillet, heat milk to simmering. Divide meringue into 6 equal portions; drop each into milk. Simmer, uncovered, till firm, about 5 minutes. Lift meringue puffs from milk (reserve milk for custard); drain meringue puffs on paper toweling. Chill well.

Meanwhile, in medium saucepan beat egg and egg yolks slightly; add remaining sugar and salt. Stir in reserved, slightly cooled milk. Cook and stir over low heat till mixture thickens slightly and coats a metal spoon. Remove from heat. Cool custard quickly by setting pan in cold water and stirring mixture a few minutes. Stir in vanilla. Place peach slices in serving dish; pour custard over. Top with meringue puffs. Makes 6 servings.

Desserts from the Freezer

CRAN-HONEYDEW PARFAITS

51 calories/serving

1 cup fresh cranberries
1 cup low-calorie cranberry
   juice cocktail
1 cup low-calorie lemon-lime
   carbonated beverage
2½ cups honeydew melon balls

In saucepan combine cranberries and cranberry juice cocktail. Heat to boiling; boil 5 minutes. Reduce heat; simmer till a drop of sauce jells on a cold plate, about 5 minutes. Cool. Slowly pour carbonated beverage into cranberry sauce. Mix gently. Pour into 4-cup freezer tray; freeze till firm. Break cranberry mixture into chunks; place in chilled bowl. Beat fluffy. Return to tray; freeze firm.

To serve, alternate layers of honeydew melon balls and small scoops of cranberry sherbet in 6 parfait glasses. Makes 6 servings.

A frozen low-calorie dessert has added eye appeal if it is molded. To make a two-layered bombe, quickly spread the first layer up the sides of the mold with the back of a chilled spoon. Freeze till firm, then fill with the second layer.

PLUM-MACAROON BOMBE

128 calories/serving

Drain one 16-ounce can purple plums (calories reduced), reserving syrup. Pit plums. Puree plums with syrup in blender. In saucepan combine 1 envelope unflavored gelatin and 2 tablespoons sugar. Add purée. Stir over low heat till gelatin dissolves. Add ½ teaspoon almond extract and a few drops red food coloring. Pour into freezer tray; freeze till firm.

Prepare 1 envelope from a 2½-ounce package low-calorie dessert topping mix following package directions. Break plum mixture in chunks; place in chilled bowl. Beat with electric mixer till smooth. Fold in *half* the topping. Pour into chilled 4½-cup metal mold. Chill till partially frozen. With chilled spoon, quickly spread mixture up sides of mold. Be sure sherbet comes to top. (If it slips down, refreeze in mold till workable.)

In saucepan combine 2 eggs, ½ cup reconstituted nonfat dry milk, and 1 teaspoon sugar. Cook and stir over low heat till mixture coats a metal spoon. Remove from heat; stir in ½ teaspoon almond extract and ¼ teaspoon vanilla. Cool. Fold in remaining topping and 2 medium macaroons, broken up. Pile custard mixture into mold, smoothing top. Cover with foil; freeze till firm. To serve, peel off foil. Invert mold on chilled plate. Rub mold with hot, damp towel to loosen; lift off mold. Garnish with fresh mint sprigs, if desired. Let stand 15 minutes before serving. Serves 8.

Mint-laden bombe

Plum-Macaroon Bombe features a creamy, maca-roon-filled frozen custard surrounded by a purple plum sherbet. A hint of almond flavors both layers. →

ORANGE ALASKAS

111 calories/serving

Pictured on pages 6 and 7 —

> 4 small oranges
> ½ cup frozen whipped dessert topping,
>   thawed
>
> • • •
>
> 1 egg white
> ⅛ teaspoon cream of tartar
> ⅛ teaspoon vanilla
> 1 tablespoon sugar
> 1 egg yolk

Cut a thin slice off bottom of each orange to make it sit flat. Cut off tops of oranges a fourth of the way down. Remove tops and discard. Carefully scoop out pulp, reserving pulp, juice, and shells; discard seeds. Place orange pulp and orange juice in blender container. Cover; blend till pureed. Stir in whipped dessert topping. Pour into 2-cup freezer tray; freeze the mixture till firm.

Just before serving, beat egg white with cream of tartar and vanilla till soft peaks form; gradually add sugar, beating till stiff peaks form. In a separate bowl, thoroughly beat egg yolk. Gently fold beaten egg yolk into stiffly beaten egg white mixture.

Break up frozen orange mixture and spoon into orange shells. Cover with meringue mixture, sealing to edges of oranges all around. Bake at 500° till lightly browned, about 2 to 3 minutes. Makes 4 servings.

Prepare smooth frozen desserts

Use interfering ingredients such as gelatin, beaten egg whites, and evaporated skim milk to minimize the ice crystals in low-calorie frozen desserts. To ensure a smooth texture, beat the mixture after it has been frozen once, then refreeze.

BANANA TORTONI

84 calories/serving

> 2 cups reconstituted nonfat dry milk
> 1 3¼-ounce package regular vanilla
>   pudding mix
> ¼ teaspoon almond extract
> 1 fully ripe medium banana, mashed
> 2 stiffly beaten egg whites
> 4 maraschino cherries, halved

Using reconstituted milk, prepare pudding following package directions. Stir in extract; cool. Fold in banana and egg whites. Pour into 8 paper bake cups in muffin pans. Freeze firm. Garnish each with cherry half. Serves 8.

APPLE-RASPBERRY FREEZE

82 calories/serving

> 1 16-ounce can applesauce (water pack)
> 1 3-ounce package Neufchâtel cheese,
>   softened
> ½ cup low-calorie raspberry jam
> 2 drops red food coloring
> 1 envelope from a 2½-ounce package
>   low-calorie dessert topping mix

Beat applesauce and cheese till smooth. Stir in jam and food coloring. Prepare topping following package directions. Fold into apple mixture. Pour into 8½x4½x2½-inch loaf dish. Freeze firm. Let stand at room temperature 10 to 15 minutes. Unmold; slice. Serves 10.

DOUBLE STRAWBERRY ICE

97 calories/serving

> 2 10-ounce packages frozen strawberries
> 1 3-ounce package regular strawberry-
>   flavored gelatin
> ¼ cup orange juice
> 1 tablespoon lemon juice

Thaw berries; sieve. Dissolve gelatin in 1 cup boiling water; stir in ¾ cup cold water, juices, and berries. Pour into two 3-cup freezer trays. Freeze firm. Break up. Beat smooth. Return to trays; freeze firm. Makes 10 servings.

FROZEN ORANGE MIST
63 calories/serving

1 6-ounce can evaporated skim milk
  (⅔ cup)
1 cup reconstituted frozen orange juice
1 tablespoon lemon juice
¼ cup sugar
¼ teaspoon grated orange peel (optional)
1 cup reconstituted nonfat dry milk

Pour evaporated milk into shallow container; freeze till ice crystals form around edges. Combine orange juice, lemon juice, sugar, and orange peel; stir till sugar dissolves. Gradually add reconstituted milk, stirring constantly. Pour into two 3-cup freezer trays; freeze till firm. Dip trays in warm water. Break frozen mixture into chunks; place in chilled bowl. Beat with electric mixer till smooth.

In chilled bowl, whip icy cold evaporated milk till stiff peaks form; fold into frozen mixture. Return to freezer trays; freeze till firm. Cut in squares. Make 8 servings.

Pink Confetti Ice is a dessert that lives up to its colorful name. Pieces of maraschino cherries speckle this pastel, triple-fruit frozen dessert.

FROSTY LEMON SQUARES
82 calories/serving

Separates into two layers —

2 egg yolks
1 teaspoon grated lemon peel
⅓ cup lemon juice
½ cup sugar
  Dash salt
2 egg whites
⅔ cup nonfat dry milk powder
⅔ cup cold water
4 coconut bar cookies, crushed

Stir together egg yolks, lemon peel, and lemon juice. Add sugar and salt; mix well. In large bowl combine egg whites, dry milk powder, and water. Beat at high speed with electric mixer to stiff peaks, about 5 minutes. Add egg yolk mixture, beating at low speed just till blended. Pour into 9x9x2-inch pan. Top with cookie crumbs. Freeze till firm. Before cutting, dip bottom of pan in warm water for 10 seconds. Cut in squares. Makes 12 servings.

PINK CONFETTI ICE
69 calories/serving

To save time, puree fruits in the blender —

½ medium cantaloupe
1 medium orange
1 medium lemon
⅓ cup evaporated skim milk
⅓ cup light corn syrup
4 maraschino cherries, chopped
  Few drops red food coloring

Remove rind from melon, orange, and lemon. Cut up fruit; remove seeds. Place fruit in blender. Cover; blend till pureed. Add 1½ cups water, milk, and corn syrup; blend well. Stir in cherries. Tint pink with food coloring. Pour into 3-cup freezer tray; freeze firm.

Break mixture into chunks; place in chilled bowl. Beat with electric mixer till smooth. Return mixture to freezer tray; cover and freeze till firm. Let stand at room temperature about 10 minutes before serving. Makes 8 servings.

PEACH AND LEMON SHERBET
75 calories/serving

This intriguing dessert obtains its delicate color from pink lemonade concentrate—

- **1 cup evaporated skim milk**
- **4 fresh medium peaches, peeled and pitted**
- **1 6-ounce can frozen pink lemonade concentrate, thawed**

Pour evaporated skim milk into shallow container; freeze till ice crystals form around edges. Puree peaches. In large bowl whip icy cold evaporated milk with electric mixer till stiff peaks form. Beat in pink lemonade concentrate and pureed peaches. Turn mixture into three 3-cup freezer trays. Freeze till nearly firm, 1 to 2 hours. Stir. Freeze mixture till firm. Makes 10 servings.

TRINIDAD BANANA SHERBET
63 calories/serving

Easy to prepare—

- **1 6-ounce can evaporated skim milk**
- **½ of 6-ounce can frozen limeade concentrate, thawed (⅓ cup)**
- **1 fully ripe medium banana, mashed (½ cup)**
- **2 tablespoons shredded coconut, toasted**
- **6 to 8 drops green food coloring**

Pour milk into shallow container; freeze till ice crystals form around edges. In chilled bowl, whip icy cold milk with electric mixer till stiff peaks form. Combine limeade concentrate, mashed banana, toasted coconut, and green food coloring; fold into whipped milk. Turn into 4-cup freezer tray; freeze till firm. Makes 8 servings.

Trinidad Banana Sherbet offers a melt-in-your-mouth taste without the unwanted calories. Just blend together limeade concentrate, mashed banana, toasted coconut, and whipped evaporated skim milk, and freeze.

RHUBARB-MALLOW FREEZE
81 calories/serving

> ¾ pound fresh rhubarb, cut in 1-inch
>   pieces (3 cups)
> ⅓ cup sugar
> ¼ cup water
> 10 marshmallows
> ½ cup evaporated skim milk
> 1 tablespoon lemon juice
> 5 drops red food coloring

In saucepan combine rhubarb pieces, sugar, and water. Bring to boiling. Reduce heat; cover and simmer till almost tender, 2 to 3 minutes. Add marshmallows; heat and stir till marshmallows dissolve. Pour into 4-cup freezer tray; freeze mixture till firm.

Meanwhile, pour evaporated milk into shallow container; freeze till ice crystals form around edges. Whip icy cold evaporated milk till soft peaks form. Break frozen rhubarb mixture into chunks; place in chilled bowl. Add lemon juice. Beat with electric mixer till fluffy. Fold in whipped milk. Tint pink with food coloring. Return to freezer tray; freeze till firm. Makes 8 servings.

STRAWBERRY-BANANA ICE
45 calories/serving

> 1 4-serving envelope low-calorie
>   strawberry-flavored gelatin
> 1 cup boiling water
> ¾ cup cold water
> 2 tablespoons lemon juice
> ¾ teaspoon rum flavoring
> 1 10-ounce package frozen
>   strawberries, thawed
> 1 fully ripe medium banana, mashed

Dissolve gelatin in boiling water; stir in cold water, lemon juice, and rum flavoring. Stir strawberries and mashed banana into gelatin. Pour mixture into two 4-cup freezer trays. Freeze till mixture is firm. Break into chunks. In chilled bowl beat *half* the mixture with electric mixer till smooth. Return to tray. Repeat with remaining mixture. Freeze the fruit mixtures till firm. Makes 10 servings.

PINEAPPLE-YOGURT FREEZE
122 calories/serving

So creamy it needs only one beating—

> 2 egg whites
> ⅓ cup sugar
> 1 cup yogurt
> 1 20-ounce can crushed pineapple
>   (juice pack), drained

Beat egg whites till soft peaks form; gradually add sugar, beating till stiff peaks form. Fold egg whites and yogurt into crushed pineapple. Pour into 3-cup freezer tray. Freeze till firm. Allow to stand at room temperature about 15 minutes before serving. To serve, cut into wedges. Makes 6 servings.

MOCHA ICE MILK
136 calories/serving

Team chocolate with coffee for a dessert so tasty, yet low in calories—

> 1 tablespoon cornstarch
> ⅓ cup water
> 1 14½-ounce can evaporated skim milk
>   (1⅔ cups)
> 3 well-beaten egg yolks
> ⅓ cup sugar
> 1 1-ounce square semisweet chocolate,
>   melted
> 2 teaspoons instant coffee powder
>   Dash salt
> 3 egg whites

In medium saucepan blend cornstarch and water; stir in evaporated milk. Cook and stir till mixture thickens and bubbles. Stir moderate amount of hot mixture into egg yolks; return to hot mixture in pan. Cook and stir over low heat 1 minute more; stir in sugar, chocolate, coffee powder, and salt. Cool thoroughly.

Beat egg whites till stiff peaks form. Fold into mocha mixture. Turn into 11x7x1½-inch pan; freeze till nearly firm. Break into chunks. In chilled bowl beat with electric mixer till smooth. Turn mixture into 3-cup freezer tray; freeze till firm. Makes 7 servings.

Treasury of Cakes and Cookies

CHOCO-MINT ROLL

128 calories/serving

Pictured on the cover—

 4 egg yolks
   Few drops red food coloring
 ¼ cup granulated sugar
 4 egg whites
 ¼ cup granulated sugar
 ½ cup sifted cake flour
 ¼ cup unsweetened cocoa powder
 1 teaspoon baking powder
 1 tablespoon sifted powdered sugar
 ⅓ cup granulated sugar
 ⅓ cup nonfat dry milk powder
 2 tablespoons cornstarch
 2 well-beaten eggs
   Few drops peppermint extract
   Few drops red food coloring

Beat yolks till thick and lemon-colored. Add food coloring. Gradually beat in ¼ cup sugar. Beat whites to soft peaks; add ¼ cup sugar, beating to stiff peaks. Fold yolks into whites. Sift together flour, cocoa, baking powder, and ¼ teaspoon salt; fold into egg mixture. Spread evenly in waxed paper-lined 15½x10½x1-inch jelly-roll pan. Bake at 375° for 10 to 12 minutes. Loosen sides; turn out on towel sprinkled with powdered sugar. Remove paper. Starting at narrow end, roll cake and towel together; cool thoroughly.

Blend ⅓ cup sugar, milk powder, cornstarch, and dash salt; add 1⅓ cups water. Stir over medium heat till bubbly; cook and stir 2 minutes. Remove from heat. Stir moderate amount of hot mixture into beaten eggs; return to hot mixture. Cook and stir 2 minutes. Remove from heat; add extract and food coloring. Cover with plastic wrap; cool. Unroll cake; spread with filling. Roll up. Serves 12.

STRAWBERRY CAKE ROLL

129 calories/serving

Worthy of high praise—

 ¾ cup sifted cake flour
 ¾ teaspoon baking powder
 ¼ teaspoon salt
 4 eggs
 1 teaspoon vanilla
 ½ cup granulated sugar
 1 tablespoon sifted powdered sugar
 1 cup boiling water
 1 4-serving envelope low-calorie
   strawberry-flavored gelatin
 1 10-ounce package frozen strawberries
 1 envelope from a 2½-ounce package
   low-calorie dessert topping mix

Sift together flour, baking powder, and salt. Beat eggs and vanilla till thick and lemon-colored. Gradually add ½ cup granulated sugar, beating till fluffy. Fold in flour mixture. Spread batter evenly in waxed paper-lined 15½x10½x1-inch jelly-roll pan. Bake at 400° till lightly browned, about 10 to 12 minutes. Immediately loosen sides; turn onto towel sprinkled with powdered sugar; remove waxed paper. Starting at narrow end, roll cake and towel together; cool 30 minutes on rack. Chill thoroughly.

Meanwhile, dissolve gelatin in 1 cup boiling water; stir in frozen strawberries till thawed. Chill till partially thickened. Unroll cake. Spread with gelatin mixture; place in refrigerator till gelatin mixture is *almost* firm, about 10 minutes. Carefully reroll cake. Chill several hours. Prepare dessert topping mix according to package directions, *except* add 1 tablespoon additional water. Frost cake roll with whipped topping. Refrigerate till serving time. Makes 12 servings.

Try a slice of luscious Strawberry Cake Roll with its bright red strawberry fruit and gelatin filling. Mouth-watering whipped dessert topping surrounds the tender cake roll, special enough for your favorite guests.

SPONGE CAKE
82 calories/serving

  1 cup sifted cake flour
1¼ cups sifted powdered sugar
  5 egg yolks
  5 egg whites
½ teaspoon cream of tartar
  1 teaspoon vanilla
½ teaspoon almond extract

Combine flour and ½ *cup* of the sugar; set aside. Beat egg yolks till thick and lemon-colored. Gradually add remaining sugar and ½ teaspoon salt, beating constantly. Wash beaters; beat egg whites with remaining ingredients to soft peaks. Gently fold yolk mixture into whites. Sift flour mixture over batter ⅓ at a time; gently fold in. Bake in *ungreased* 9-inch tube pan at 325° for 55 minutes. Invert cake in pan; cool. Makes 16 servings.

BERRY-RHUBARB SHORTCAKE
128 calories/serving

Pictured on the cover —

    1¼ cups sifted all-purpose flour
    1 tablespoon sugar
    2 teaspoons baking powder
    ¼ teaspoon baking soda
    2 tablespoons butter or margarine
    1 egg
    ⅓ cup buttermilk
    1½ cups fresh rhubarb, cut in 1-inch
        pieces
        Noncaloric sweetener to equal
        ¼ cup sugar
    ¾ cup water
    1 tablespoon cornstarch
        Dash salt
    2 tablespoons cold water
    1 teaspoon lemon juice
    1 teaspoon vanilla
    5 drops red food coloring
    1 cup fresh strawberries, sliced
    ½ cup whipped low-calorie dessert
        topping

Sift together sifted all-purpose flour, sugar, baking powder, and baking soda; cut in butter or margarine till mixture resembles coarse crumbs. Combine egg and buttermilk; add to flour mixture all at once, stirring till combined. Turn out onto lightly floured surface; knead gently for ½ minute. Roll dough into a 10x5-inch rectangle. Cut into eight 2½-inch squares. Place squares on *ungreased* baking sheet. Bake at 450° for 10 minutes.

To make filling, combine rhubarb pieces, noncaloric sweetener, and ¾ cup water in saucepan. Bring to boiling; reduce heat. Simmer till almost tender, about 2 minutes. Remove from heat. Drain, reserving syrup. Add water to syrup to make 1 cup. Mix cornstarch, dash salt, and 2 tablespoons cold water; add to syrup mixture. Cook and stir till thick and bubbly. Cook and stir 2 minutes more. Remove from heat. Stir in lemon juice, vanilla, and red food coloring. Cool slightly. Gently stir in rhubarb and strawberries. Spoon the rhubarb-strawberry mixture atop shortcake squares. Top each with topping. Serves 8.

CHIFFON CAKE
129 calories/serving

Sift together 1¾ cups sifted cake flour, 1¼ cups sifted powdered sugar, 2 teaspoons baking powder, and ½ teaspoon salt into bowl; mix well. Add in order: ¼ cup salad oil, 4 egg yolks, ⅓ cup water, 1 teaspoon vanilla, 2 teaspoons grated lemon peel, and ¼ teaspoon lemon extract. Beat till satin smooth. Beat 6 egg whites with ½ teaspoon cream of tartar till *very stiff peaks* form. Fold egg whites gently into yolk mixture. Bake in *ungreased* 9-inch tube pan at 325° till done, about 55 minutes. Invert pan; cool. Serves 16.

ANGEL CAKE
76 calories/serving

Sift 1 cup sifted cake flour with ½ cup sifted powdered sugar 2 times; set flour mixture aside. In large mixer bowl beat 10 egg whites (1¼ cups) with 1½ teaspoons cream of tartar, ¼ teaspoon salt, and 1½ teaspoons vanilla till soft peaks form but are still moist and glossy. Add 1 cup sifted powdered sugar, 2 tablespoons at a time, continuing to beat till the egg whites hold *very stiff* peaks.

Sift about ¼ of flour mixture over whites; fold in. Repeat, folding in remaining flour by fourths. Bake in *ungreased* 9-inch tube pan at 375° till done, about 30 to 35 minutes. Invert cake in pan; cool. Makes 16 servings.

CHOCOLATE ANGEL CAKE
80 calories/serving

Prepare Angel Cake, sifting 3 tablespoons unsweetened cocoa powder with flour and sugar 2 times. Makes 16 servings.

MOCHA ANGEL CAKE
82 calories/serving

Prepare Angel Cake, sifting ¼ cup unsweetened cocoa powder and 1 tablespoon instant coffee powder with the flour and powdered sugar 2 times. Makes 16 servings.

BUTTERSCOTCH THINS
42 calories/cookie

½ cup butter or margarine
⅔ cup brown sugar
½ teaspoon vanilla
1 egg
1½ cups sifted all-purpose flour
1½ teaspoons baking powder

Cream first 3 ingredients till light and fluffy; beat in egg. Sift together dry ingredients and ¼ teaspoon salt; mix into creamed mixture. Divide dough into 4 parts; make 12 balls about ½ inch in diameter out of each part. Place balls on ungreased cookie sheet. Flatten by crisscrossing with fork tines. Bake at 375° for 7 to 8 minutes. Makes 4 dozen.

OATMEAL CRUNCHIES
30 calories/cookie

Sift together ½ cup sifted all-purpose flour, ¼ cup granulated sugar, ½ teaspoon baking powder, ½ teaspoon baking soda, and ¼ teaspoon salt. Add ¼ cup brown sugar, ¼ cup butter, 1 egg, 2 tablespoons yogurt, and ¼ teaspoon vanilla; beat well.

Stir in 1 cup quick-cooking rolled oats. Chill dough. Drop from teaspoon onto ungreased cookie sheet. Bake at 375° for about 8 minutes. Cool slightly before removing from cookie sheet. Makes 4 dozen cookies.

COCONUT MERINGUE COOKIES
45 calories/cookie

Chewy bits of coconut in a delicate cookie—

2 egg whites
½ teaspoon vanilla
½ cup sugar
1 cup flaked coconut

Beat whites with dash salt and vanilla to soft peaks. Gradually add sugar; beat to stiff peaks. Fold in coconut. Drop by rounded tablespoons onto greased cookie sheet. Bake at 325° about 20 minutes. Makes 2 dozen.

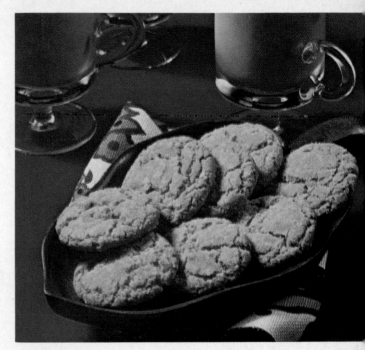

Crinkle-topped Gingersnaps with a sprinkling of sugar are perfect for a snack or noontime luncheon. They're a favorite with both children and adults.

GINGERSNAPS
41 calories/cookie

½ cup shortening
¼ cup brown sugar
3 tablespoons molasses
1 egg
1¼ cups sifted all-purpose flour
1 teaspoon baking soda
½ teaspoon ground ginger
½ teaspoon ground cinnamon
¼ teaspoon ground cloves
3 tablespoons granulated sugar

Cream first 4 ingredients till fluffy. Sift together flour, soda, ¼ teaspoon salt, ginger, cinnamon, and cloves; stir into molasses mixture. Chill dough. Using 1 heaping teaspoon mixture for each cookie, form in 1-inch balls. Roll in granulated sugar; place 2 inches apart on lightly greased cookie sheet. Bake at 375° for 10 to 12 minutes. Makes 4 dozen.

Memorable Pies

BLUEBERRY-LEMON CHEESE PIE
132 calories/serving

A no-bake cheesecake pie topped with saucy blueberries—

> 1 cup dry cottage cheese
> 1 envelope unflavored gelatin
>   Noncaloric sweetener to equal
>   ⅓ cup sugar
> 1 cup cold water
> 1 teaspoon grated lemon peel
> 3 tablespoons lemon juice
> 6 drops yellow food coloring
> 2 egg whites
> 1 9-inch Graham Cracker Crust
>   (page 43)
>   • • •
> 1 9-ounce carton frozen unsweetened
>   blueberries, thawed
> 1 tablespoon cornstarch
> ½ cup cold water
>   Noncaloric sweetener to equal
>   1 tablespoon sugar
> ¼ teaspoon vanilla

Press cottage cheese through sieve. In saucepan combine gelatin, noncaloric sweetener to equal ⅓ cup sugar, and 1 cup water. Cook and stir over medium heat till gelatin dissolves. Remove from heat. Add sieved cottage cheese, lemon peel, lemon juice, and yellow food coloring; beat with electric mixer till smooth. Chill till partially set. Beat egg whites to stiff peaks; fold into gelatin mixture. Pour into Graham Cracker Crust. Chill till firm.

In saucepan crush ½ *cup* blueberries. Blend together cornstarch and ½ cup cold water. Add constarch mixture and noncaloric sweetener to equal 1 tablespoon sugar to crushed blueberries. Cook over medium heat, stirring constantly, till mixture is thick and bubbly; cook and stir 1 minute longer. Remove from heat; stir in remaining blueberries and vanilla. Cool. Pour sauce over pie, spreading to edge of pie. Chill. Makes 8 servings.

ORANGE CHIFFON PIE
144 calories/serving

Pleasing citrus flavor in a fluffy chiffon pie with special Egg Pastry shell—

> 1 envelope unflavored gelatin
>   Dash salt
> 1 cup orange juice
> ¼ cup cold water
>   Noncaloric sweetener to equal
>   ¼ cup sugar
> 3 beaten egg yolks
>   • • •
> ¼ teaspoon grated orange peel
> 6 drops yellow food coloring
> 2 drops red food coloring
> 3 egg whites
>   • • •
> 1 baked 8-inch Egg Pastry shell
>   (page 43)
> ½ cup whipped low-calorie dessert
>   topping
>   Shredded orange peel

In saucepan combine unflavored gelatin, salt, orange juice, cold water, and noncaloric sweetener. Stir in beaten egg yolks. Cook and stir over medium heat till mixture thickens slightly, about 2 to 3 minutes. Remove from heat; stir in orange peel and yellow and red food coloring. Chill, stirring occasionally, till mixture mounds slightly when spooned.

Beat egg whites till stiff peaks form. Fold into gelatin mixture. Pile into cooled, baked Egg Pastry shell. Chill till firm. Garnish with dollops of whipped dessert topping and shredded orange peel. Makes 8 servings.

A pie to delight dieters

*Serve your family Orange Chiffon Pie, and watch →
your weight at the same time. Both piecrust and
filling have been adapted for calorie counters.*

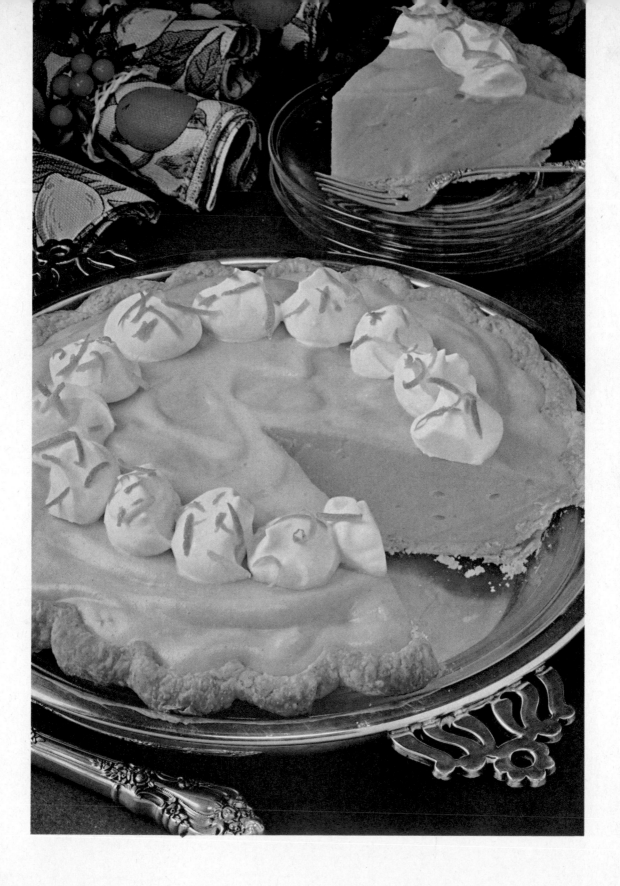

PEAR-LIME CHIFFON PIE
138 calories/serving

Drain one 16-ounce can pear halves (water pack), reserving liquid and 1 pear half. Chop remaining pears. Blend one 4-serving envelope low-calorie lime-flavored gelatin and dash salt; stir in pear liquid, ½ cup cold water, and 1 tablespoon lime juice. Let stand a few minutes. Cook and stir till gelatin dissolves. Stir moderate amount of hot mixture into 3 beaten egg yolks. Return to saucepan; cook 2 minutes more. Stir in chopped pears. Chill gelatin mixture till partially set.

Beat 3 egg whites, 1 teaspoon vanilla, and ¼ teaspoon cream of tartar to stiff peaks. Fold in gelatin, Chill, if necessary, till mixture mounds when spooned. Turn into one cooled, *baked* 8-inch Yogurt Pastry shell (page 43); chill till firm. Top with ¼ cup *whipped* low-calorie dessert topping and reserved pear half, sliced. Makes 8 servings.

For added appeal, decorate the center of fluffy Pear-Lime Chiffon Pie with a mound of low-calorie dessert topping and a sliced pear spiral.

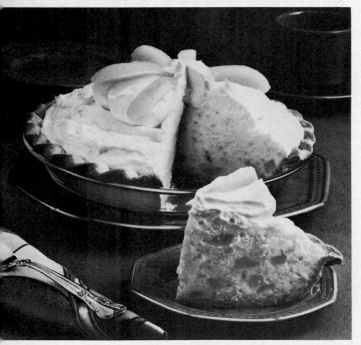

TANGY LIME PIE
140 calories/serving

Pictured on the cover—

   1 envelope unflavored gelatin
      Noncaloric sweetener to equal
         ½ cup sugar
   ¼ cup lime juice
   3 well-beaten egg yolks
   ½ teaspoon grated lime peel
   4 to 6 drops green food coloring
   3 egg whites
   ¼ teaspoon cream of tartar
   1 cup whipped low-calorie dessert
      topping
   1 baked 9-inch Cottage Cheese Pastry
      shell (page 43)

Mix first 3 ingredients. Beat yolks and 1 cup cold water together; stir into gelatin. Cook and stir just to boiling. Remove from heat; stir in peel and food coloring. Chill, stirring occasionally, till mixture begins to set. Beat whites with cream of tartar to stiff peaks. Fold into gelatin. Fold in topping; chill till mixture mounds. Pile into cooled shell. Garnish with lime slices, if desired. Serves 8.

PINEAPPLE DREAM PIE
141 calories/serving

Combine ¾ cup flaked coconut and 1 tablespoon butter or margarine; press on bottom and sides of 9-inch pie plate. Bake at 325° till golden, about 15 minutes; cool.

Using 1¼ cups from a 20-ounce can crushed pineapple (juice pack), drain pineapple, reserving juice. Add water to juice to make ¾ cup. In saucepan soften 1 envelope unflavored gelatin in pineapple juice. Heat and stir till gelatin dissolves; stir in 2 tablespoons lemon juice. Chill till partially set.

Using 2 cups reconstituted nonfat dry milk, prepare one 4-serving envelope low-calorie vanilla pudding mix following package directions; cool. Whip partially set gelatin till fluffy; fold in pudding and pineapple. Pour into crust. Chill till firm. Garnish with ½ cup *whipped* low-calorie dessert topping. Serves 8.

GRAHAM CRACKER CRUST
624 calories/crust

> ¾ **cup graham cracker crumbs**
> 3 **tablespoons butter, melted**

Combine graham cracker crumbs and butter or margarine. Press mixture firmly into 8- or 9-inch pie plate. Chill at least 45 minutes. Makes one 8- or 9-inch crust.

GRAHAM-ZWIEBACK CRUST
925 calories/crust

> ½ **cup graham cracker crumbs**
> ½ **cup zwieback crumbs**
> 2 **tablespoons sugar**
> ¼ **cup butter or margarine, melted**

Combine graham cracker crumbs, zwieback crumbs, sugar, and butter or margarine. Press firmly into an 8- or 9-inch pie plate. Bake at 375° till edges are browned, 7 to 8 minutes; cool. *Or* for unbaked crust, chill at least 45 minutes. Makes one 8- or 9-inch crust.

EGG PASTRY
716 calories/shell

> ⅔ **cup sifted all-purpose flour**
> ¼ **teaspoon salt**
> 3 **tablespoons shortening**
> 1 **beaten egg**
> ½ **teaspoon vinegar**

Sift flour and salt together; cut in shortening with pastry blender till pieces are the size of small peas. Combine beaten egg and vinegar; add to flour-shortening mixture. Gently toss with fork till all of dough is moistened. Form dough into a ball.

Flatten dough on *very slightly* floured surface by pressing with edge of hands 3 times across in both directions. Roll from center to edge till ⅛ inch thick. Fit pastry into 8- or 9-inch pie plate; flute edges. Prick bottom and sides well with fork. Bake at 450° till crust is golden, about 10 to 12 minutes. Makes one 8- or 9-inch pastry shell.

YOGURT PASTRY
662 calories/shell

> ⅔ **cup sifted all-purpose flour**
> 3 **tablespoons shortening**
> 3 **tablespoons yogurt**

Sift flour and ¼ teaspoon salt together; cut in shortening till pieces are the size of small peas. Add yogurt. Gently stir with fork till all the mixture is moistened. Form into a ball. Flatten dough on lightly floured surface. Roll ⅛ inch thick. Fit pastry into 8-inch pie plate; flute edges. Prick well with fork. Bake at 450° till golden, about 10 minutes. Makes one 8-inch pastry shell.

COTTAGE CHEESE PASTRY
718 calories/shell

> ⅔ **cup sifted all-purpose flour**
> 3 **tablespoons shortening**
> ⅓ **cup cream-style cottage cheese, sieved**

Sift flour and ¼ teaspoon salt together; cut in shortening till pieces are the size of small peas. Add cottage cheese. Toss with fork till all is moistened. Form into a ball. Flatten on *very slightly* floured surface by pressing with edge of hands 3 times across in both directions. Roll ⅛ inch thick. Fit into 8- or 9-inch pie plate; flute edges. Prick well with fork. Bake at 450° for 10 to 12 minutes. Makes one 8- or 9-inch pastry shell.

Remove crumb crust pies easily

To loosen a crumb crust so that each piece of pie slips out neatly, wrap a hot, damp towel under the bottom and around the sides of the pie plate just before serving. Hold the towel against the plate for a few minutes. Then, cut and serve.

Desserts to Drink

SPICED HOT COCOA
98 calories/serving

Served with a whipped milk topper—

- ¼ cup unsweetened cocoa powder
- 2 tablespoons sugar
- 6 inches stick cinnamon
- 6 whole cloves
- 1⅓ cups nonfat dry milk powder
- ¼ teaspoon vanilla
- ⅓ cup nonfat dry milk powder
- ⅓ cup ice water

In a saucepan mix unsweetened cocoa powder, sugar, and dash salt; add stick cinnamon, cloves, and 1 cup water. Bring to boiling, stirring constantly. Simmer for 5 minutes.

Reconstitute 1⅓ cups nonfat dry milk powder in 3 cups water. Add to chocolate mixture. Bring just to boiling; stir in vanilla. Remove cinnamon sticks and cloves.

In mixing bowl combine ⅓ cup nonfat dry milk powder and ⅓ cup ice water; beat at high speed with electric mixer to stiff peaks.

Pour hot cocoa into 6 heatproof mugs; top with whipped milk. Serve with additional cinnamon stick stirrers, if desired. Serves 6.

Use low-calorie beverages

The calorie counts of desserts can be reduced by using diet or low-calorie carbonated beverages. The calorie counts for low-calorie carbonated beverages vary from a fraction of a calorie to 6 or 7 calories per ounce. Regular carbonated beverages, on the other hand, average 10 to 15 calories per ounce.

VANILLA MILK SHAKE
59 calories/serving

UNDER **60** CALORIES

- ½ cup evaporated skim milk
- ½ cup cold water
- 2 tablespoons frozen whipped dessert topping
- 1 teaspoon vanilla
- 6 ice cubes

In blender container combine evaporated skim milk, water, dessert topping, and vanilla. Add ice cubes, one at a time, blending at lowest speed till slushy. Makes 2 servings.

CHOCOLATE MILK SHAKE
108 calories/serving

Prepare Vanilla Milk Shake, adding 2 tablespoons chocolate syrup to milk. Serves 2.

STRAWBERRY MILK SHAKE
105 calories/serving with sugar
73 calories/serving with noncaloric sweetener

Prepare Vanilla Milk Shake, adding ½ cup frozen, whole, unsweetened strawberries and 4 teaspoons sugar *or* noncaloric sweetener to equal 4 teaspoons sugar with ice. Serves 2.

LEMONY BUTTERMILK FRAPPÉ
65 calories/serving

Quick lemon beverage with a buttermilk tang—

With electric mixer or in blender container whip 2 cups buttermilk, 1½ teaspoons grated lemon peel, 2 tablespoons lemon juice, 2 tablespoons sugar, and 6 drops yellow food coloring until frothy. Fold 1 cup *whipped* low-calorie dessert topping into buttermilk mixture; pour into six chilled glasses. Serve beverage immediately. Makes 6 servings.

CAPPUCCINO-STYLE CIDER

81 calories/serving

- 2¼ cups apple cider or juice
- ½ teaspoon whole allspice
- ½ teaspoon whole cloves
- ¼ cup frozen whipped dessert topping, thawed
- ¼ teaspoon grated orange peel
- 4 cinnamon stick stirrers

In saucepan combine cider, allspice, cloves, and dash salt; bring to boiling. Reduce heat; simmer, covered, for 20 minutes. Combine dessert topping and orange peel. Strain cider. Pour into 4 heatproof cups. Top each serving with dessert topping. Serve with cinnamon stick stirrers. Makes 4 servings.

RASPBERRY CRUSH

51 calories/serving

UNDER 60 CALORIES

- 1 10-ounce package frozen raspberries, thawed
- 3 12-ounce cans low-calorie lemon-lime carbonated beverage
- 1 envelope unsweetened raspberry-flavored soft drink powder

Thaw berries. Freeze carbonated beverage till partially frozen; break up and crush. Reserve a few berries; pour remaining berries and drink powder into blender. Add crushed beverage, 1 cup at a time. Cover; blend smooth. Stop blender occasionally and scrape sides. Spoon into glasses; garnish with berries. Top with mint, if desired. Serves 6.

Take a break from traditional everyday desserts and indulge in a delightful, drinkable dessert. Choose from such easy beverages as Raspberry Crush, Vanilla Milk Shake, and Cappuccino-Style Cider.

Flavorful Sauces and Toppings

HOMEMADE YOGURT
7 calories/tablespoon

Heat 2 cups skim milk to just below boiling (200°). Cool to 115°. In bowl blend milk with 2 tablespoons yogurt. Cover with plastic wrap. Place bowl in a larger bowl of warm water (115°) and cover with a towel or put in a warm place. Allow to stand till mixture is firm when shaken gently, 6 to 8 hours. (Change water in large bowl once or twice during this time, keeping temperature about 115°.) Remove 2 tablespoons of mixture and put in custard cup to use as starter next time. Chill yogurt and yogurt starter. Makes 2 cups.

Fruit Yogurt: (Calorie count varies with fruit used.) Heat 2 cups skim milk; add 2 tablespoons yogurt or starter. Remove 2 tablespoons of heated mixture to use as starter next time. To remaining mixture, add ¼ cup crushed, fresh or frozen fruit and 2 tablespoons sugar. Allow to stand in larger bowl of warm water till firm. Chill. Makes 2 cups.

Whipped toppings with fewer calories

Reduce the calories per tablespoon of regular whipped topping by increasing its volume. In Cool Dessert Topping and Fluffy Dessert Topping above, unflavored gelatin dissolved in a small amount of liquid is either whipped and folded into the topping or whipped along with the topping. This increases the volume as much as two times.

COOL DESSERT TOPPING
10 calories/tablespoon

In saucepan soften ½ teaspoon unflavored gelatin in ⅔ cup water; stir over low heat till gelatin dissolves. Chill till partially set. Beat with electric mixer till double in volume. Add 1 cup frozen whipped dessert topping, thawed; beat to soft peaks. Chill. Stir gently before serving. Makes 1⅔ cups.

FLUFFY DESSERT TOPPING
8 calories/tablespoon

In saucepan soften 1 teaspoon unflavored gelatin in ⅔ cup water; stir over low heat till gelatin dissolves. Cool. Prepare one 2-ounce package *regular* dessert topping mix according to package directions, *except* use ½ cup reconstituted nonfat dry milk. Stir gelatin and 1 teaspoon vanilla into dessert topping; beat to soft peaks. Cover; chill. Makes 3½ cups.

PEACHY CRANBERRY SAUCE
16 calories/tablespoon

1 8-ounce can peach slices (juice pack)
¼ cup sugar
2 tablespoons lemon juice
½ teaspoon whole cloves
3 inches stick cinnamon
½ cup fresh cranberries

Drain peaches, reserving juice. Dice peaches. Add water to juice to make 1 cup. Combine juice with next 4 ingredients; bring to boil. Simmer 5 minutes. Add cranberries; boil till skins pop, 5 minutes. Remove spices; add peaches. Cool. Cover; chill. Serve over cake, pudding, or sherbet. Makes 1¼ cups.

CHOCOLATE SAUCE
22 calories/tablespoon

Melt ¼ of a 4-ounce bar sweet cooking chocolate in a custard cup placed in a pan containing a small amount of boiling water. In medium saucepan blend 1 tablespoon sugar, 1 tablespoon cornstarch, and dash salt; stir in 1¼ cups reconstituted nonfat dry milk. Cook over low heat till mixture thickens and bubbles. Blend in chocolate. Remove from heat; stir in 1 teaspoon butter or margarine and 1 teaspoon vanilla. Chill. Makes 1 cup.

CITRUS-CHEESE TOPPER
14 calories/tablespoon

  1 3-ounce package Neufchâtel cheese, softened
  3 tablespoons sugar
  1 teaspoon grated orange peel
  ½ teaspoon grated lemon peel
  1 tablespoon orange juice
  1 tablespoon lemon juice
  ⅓ cup nonfat dry milk powder

Beat first 6 ingredients till smooth. In mixing bowl combine milk powder and ⅓ cup ice water; beat to stiff peaks. Fold into cheese mixture. (Don't overstir.) Chill. Serve over cake, pudding, or fruit. Makes 2 cups.

LIME FLUFF
4 calories/tablespoon

  ½ teaspoon unflavored gelatin
  1 tablespoon sugar
  ½ cup evaporated skim milk
  4 to 5 drops green food coloring
  1 tablespoon bottled sweetened lime juice
  1 teaspoon grated lime peel

In saucepan combine gelatin and sugar; stir in evaporated milk. Stir over low heat till gelatin dissolves. Tint with food coloring. Freeze till icy cold; whip to stiff peaks. Beat in lime juice. Spoon topping over dessert; garnish with lime peel. Makes 2 cups topping.

COFFEE ROYALE SAUCE
17 calories/tablespoon

Flavorful sauce with a hint of rum—

  ⅓ cup sugar
  1 tablespoon cornstarch
  2 teaspoons instant coffee powder
  1 cup water
  ¾ teaspoon rum flavoring

Combine sugar, cornstarch, and instant coffee powder. Stir in water. Cook, stirring constantly, over medium heat till mixture is thick and bubbly. Remove from heat; stir in rum flavoring. Serve warm with low-calorie cake, pudding, or custard. Makes 1⅛ cups sauce.

You won't have to miss the frosting when you top a slice of Mocha Angel Cake (page 38) with a dollop of Lime Fluff garnished with grated lime peel.

low-calorie desserts
FOR ENTERTAINING

When entertaining, most people want to serve a dessert that has eye appeal and lavish taste—something extra-special. All of the dessert recipes in this section have the above two features, plus they are low in calories. The chocolate-topped Coffee Meringues pictured here are a case in point. They taste as smooth, creamy, and delicious as they look.

Company-Pleasing Finales

BERRY-NECTARINE FLAMBÉ
95 calories/serving

> 3 cups fresh strawberries
> 2 tablespoons sugar
> 2 teaspoons cornstarch
> ½ of 6-ounce can frozen pineapple-
>   orange juice concentrate, thawed
>   (⅓ cup)
> ½ cup cold water
> 2 or 3 drops red food coloring
> 2 fresh medium nectarines, peeled
>   and sliced
> ½ teaspoon grated orange peel
> 2 tablespoons rum

Mash ½ *cup* berries; halve remaining berries. In blazer pan of chafing dish, combine sugar and cornstarch; gradually stir in mashed berries, concentrate, water, and food coloring. Cook and stir over medium heat till thickened and bubbly. Add halved berries, nectarines, and peel. Return to boiling. Warm rum in ladle. Ignite and pour over fruit. When flame dies, spoon fruit into serving dishes. Serves 6.

Flame a dessert for company

For a spectacular meal ending without extra calories, serve a fruit flambé in a chafing dish. To flame, pour 2 tablespoons spirits such as brandy into a ladle. Warm over a burner, then ignite spirits with a match, and pour over the dessert. When the flame dies, the alcohol has evaporated, leaving a subtle spirits flavor.

CRAN-TANGERINE MERINGUE
113 calories/serving

Pictured on the cover—

> ¼ cup sugar
> 1 teaspoon unflavored gelatin
>   Dash salt
> 1½ cups low-calorie cranberry juice
>   cocktail
> 1 teaspoon lemon juice
> 1 teaspoon unflavored gelatin
> 1 cup low-calorie lemon-lime
>   carbonated beverage
> ½ of 6-ounce can frozen tangerine juice
>   concentrate, thawed (⅓ cup)
>   Meringue Shell (page 52)

In saucepan combine first 3 ingredients. Stir in ½ *cup* cranberry juice. Stir over low heat till gelatin dissolves; remove from heat. Stir in remaining cranberry juice and lemon juice. Pour into freezer tray; freeze till firm.

In saucepan soften 1 teaspoon gelatin in carbonated beverage. Stir over low heat till gelatin dissolves. Remove from heat. Stir in tangerine juice. Pour into another freezer tray; freeze till firm.

Break *both* ices into small pieces with fork. Transfer ices to separate chilled bowls and beat with electric mixer till smooth. Return to freezer trays; freeze till firm. To serve, fill Meringue Shell with scoops of tangerine and cranberry ices. Makes 8 servings.

A sensational idea

Guests will rave about glamorous Berry-Nectarine Flambé. The fresh fruits are blended with a pineapple-orange sauce that is subtly flavored with rum. →

PEACH-ORANGE TORTE
119 calories/serving

Pictured on the contents page—

  2 tablespoons butter or margarine
  ½ cup sifted powdered sugar
  1 egg
  ½ teaspoon vanilla
  ¾ cup sifted cake flour
  1 teaspoon baking powder
  ¼ teaspoon salt
  ⅓ cup reconstituted nonfat dry milk
  1 envelope unflavored gelatin
  ¼ cup granulated sugar
  1 envelope unsweetened orange-
      flavored soft drink powder
  2 fresh medium peaches
  ½ cup whipped low-calorie dessert
      topping

Cream butter. Add powdered sugar; beat till light. Add egg and vanilla; beat till fluffy. Sift flour with baking powder and salt. Add to egg mixture alternately with milk, beating well after each addition. Spread in lightly greased and floured 8-inch springform pan; bake at 350° about 20 minutes. Cool in pan.

In saucepan combine gelatin, granulated sugar, and drink powder; stir in ½ cup cold water. Stir over low heat till gelatin dissolves. Stir in 1¼ cups cold water. Chill till partially set. Peel, pit, and slice peaches; arrange atop cooled cake. Pour gelatin over; chill till firm. Remove cake from pan; place on serving plate. Garnish with topping. Serves 10.

STRAWBERRY COMPOTE
60 calories/serving

  1 quart fresh strawberries
  2 tablespoons sugar
  ½ cup vanilla ice milk
  ½ cup yogurt

UNDER **60** *CALORIES*

Mash ¾ *cup* strawberries; stir in sugar. Halve remaining berries; spoon into a large compote or individual sherbet dishes. Stir ice milk just to soften; fold in yogurt and mashed berries. Drizzle sauce over berries. Makes 8 servings.

COFFEE MERINGUES
119 calories/serving

Pictured on pages 48 and 49—

    Individual Meringue Shells
  3 beaten egg yolks
  ¼ cup sugar
  ¼ cup reconstituted nonfat dry milk
  2 teaspoons instant coffee powder
  1 envelope from a 2½-ounce package
      low-calorie dessert topping mix
  1 stiffly beaten egg white
  1 1-ounce square sweet chocolate

Prepare Individual Meringue Shells, *except* pipe 10 shells, 2½ inches in diameter, through star pastry tube (or drop and shape with spoon) onto plain paper. Bake as directed. Cool.

In small saucepan combine egg yolks, sugar, milk, coffee powder, and dash salt. Cook over low heat, stirring constantly, till mixture coats a metal spoon. Cool thoroughly.

Prepare topping mix following package directions. Fold topping and egg white into custard mixture. Chill. Spoon into meringue shells. Shave chocolate; sprinkle over. Serves 10.

MERINGUE SHELL
417 calories/shell

Have 2 egg whites at room temperature. Add ½ teaspoon vanilla, ¼ teaspoon cream of tartar, and dash salt. Beat to soft peaks. *Gradually* add ½ cup sugar, beating till very stiff peaks form and sugar is dissolved. Cover baking sheet with plain brown paper. Draw 9-inch round circle on paper. Spread meringue over circle. Shape into shell with back of spoon, making sides higher. Bake at 275° for 50 minutes. Turn off heat. Let dry in oven (door closed) at least 2 hours. Makes one 9-inch shell.

Individual Meringue Shells: (52 calories/shell) Prepare meringue as for Meringue Shell. Cover baking sheet with plain brown paper. Draw 8 circles, 3 inches in diameter; spread each with meringue. Using back of spoon, shape into shells. Bake at 275° for 50 minutes. For crisper meringues turn off heat. Dry in oven (door closed) about 1 hour. Makes 8 shells.

PINEAPPLE AMBROSIA BOAT
114 calories/serving

1 fresh medium pineapple (2 pounds)
⅓ cup snipped dried apricots
3 medium macaroons, crumbled
¼ cup low-calorie peach preserves
½ teaspoon rum flavoring

Wash pineapple. Using sharp knife, make a lengthwise slice, cutting off about ¼ of pineapple. With grapefruit or paring knife, remove fruit from both shells, leaving ½-inch sides. Discard smaller shell. Cut fruit in chunks, discarding center core. Cover apricots with hot water. Let stand 5 minutes; drain.

Combine fruit chunks, apricots, and macaroons. Mix preserves and flavoring; toss with fruit. Put shell in shallow baking dish; spoon fruit into shell. Cover shell and crown with foil. Bake at 350° for 40 minutes. Uncover fruit (not crown); bake 15 minutes. Serves 6.

ALMOND-PINEAPPLE BAKE
115 calories/serving

1 20-ounce can pineapple chunks (juice pack), cut up
1 tablespoon cornstarch
1 beaten egg yolk
1 teaspoon vanilla
¼ teaspoon almond extract
1 egg white
¼ teaspoon cream of tartar
2 tablespoons brown sugar
1 tablespoon slivered almonds, toasted

Drain pineapple, reserving juice. In saucepan gradually blend reserved juice into cornstarch; cook and stir till thickened and bubbly. Stir about half of juice mixture into egg yolk; return to saucepan. Cook and stir over low heat just till bubbly. Remove from heat; stir in vanilla, extract, and pineapple.

Beat egg white with cream of tartar till soft peaks form. Gradually add brown sugar, beating to stiff peaks. Pour pineapple mixture into 1-quart casserole; top with meringue. Bake at 350° for 15 to 20 minutes. Garnish with almonds. Serve warm. Makes 5 servings.

FORGOTTEN CHERRY TORTE
126 calories/serving

Luscious cherry filling is layered between crispy meringue and smooth whipped topping—

Preheat oven to 450°. In bowl combine 4 egg whites, ½ cup sugar, and ¼ teaspoon cream of tartar. Beat at high speed with electric mixer till *very stiff* peaks form, about 15 minutes. Spread on bottom and sides of 9-inch pie plate. Do not build sides above plate. Place in preheated oven; turn off heat immediately. Let stand in oven *with door closed* for 5 hours or overnight. *Do not open oven door.*

Drain one 16-ounce can dark sweet cherries (water pack), reserving liquid. Pit cherries. In saucepan combine 2 tablespoons cornstarch, 1 tablespoon sugar, and dash salt; stir in cherry liquid. Cook and stir till thick and bubbly; remove from heat. Stir in cherries and ½ teaspoon almond extract. Cover; cool.

Prepare 1 envelope from a 2¼-ounce package low-calorie dessert topping mix according to package directions. Spread cherry filling evenly in meringue shell. Spread topping over filling to cover edges of meringue. Chill 4 hours or overnight. Makes 8 servings.

MELON-CHERRY FONDUE
129 calories/serving

1 cup honeydew melon balls
1 cup cantaloupe balls
1 cup watermelon balls
1 16-ounce can dark sweet cherries (water pack)
¼ cup sugar
2 tablespoons cornstarch
1 teaspoon lemon juice
1 teaspoon brandy flavoring

Divide melon balls into 6 serving dishes; let stand at room temperature. Pit cherries. In blender container combine undrained cherries, sugar, and cornstarch; blend till smooth. Cook and stir till thickened and bubbly. Stir in lemon juice and brandy flavoring. Pour into fondue pot; place over fondue burner. Spear fruit with fondue fork; dip in sauce. Serves 6.

MILK CHOCOLATE FREEZE
129 calories/serving

Tastes like a fudge-flavored ice cream bar—

> 24 vanilla wafers, crushed (1 cup)
> 1½ cups reconstituted nonfat dry milk
> 1 3¾-ounce package regular milk chocolate pudding mix
> 2 egg yolks
> 2 stiffly beaten egg whites
> 1 envelope from a 2½-ounce package low-calorie dessert topping mix

Line bottom of 11¾x7½x1¾-inch baking dish with ¾ *cup* of the vanilla wafer crumbs. Using the 1½ cups reconstituted nonfat dry milk, prepare pudding mix following package directions. Stir a moderate amount of hot pudding into egg yolks; return to pudding in pan. Cook and stir till thickened and bubbly. Cover surface with waxed paper; cool.

Fold egg whites into cooled pudding. Spoon carefully into prepared pan; spread evenly. Prepare topping mix following package directions; spread gently and evenly over pudding mixture. Sprinkle top with remaining wafer crumbs. Freeze till firm, about 3 hours. Remove from freezer 5 to 10 minutes before serving. Cut in squares. Makes 10 servings.

FROZEN MAPLE DESSERT
150 calories/serving

Pureed cottage cheese provides the tanginess—

> 1½ cups cream-style cottage cheese
> ⅓ cup brown sugar
> 1 egg
> 8 drops maple flavoring
> 1 pint vanilla ice milk
> 2 tablespoons flaked coconut, toasted

Place cottage cheese, brown sugar, egg, and maple flavoring in blender container; cover and blend till smooth. In large chilled bowl stir vanilla ice milk just to soften; fold in cottage cheese mixture. Pour into 8x8x2-inch pan. Cover and freeze till firm. Sprinkle with coconut before serving. Makes 8 servings.

STRAWBERRY RIBBON PIE
134 calories/serving

> 2 4-serving envelopes low-calorie strawberry-flavored gelatin
> 1 tablespoon lemon juice
> 1 9-inch Graham Cracker Crust (page 43)
> 2 cups fresh strawberries, mashed
> 2 egg whites
> ¼ teaspoon cream of tartar
> 1 envelope from a 2½-ounce package low-calorie dessert topping mix
> 1 teaspoon skim milk

Dissolve gelatin in 2 cups boiling water; add lemon juice. Measure ½ *cup* dissolved gelatin; stir in ½ cup cold water. Chill till partially set. Turn into Graham Cracker Crust; chill till *almost* firm. To the remaining 1½ cups gelatin, add ½ cup cold water; chill till partially set. Fold in strawberries. Beat egg whites and cream of tartar to stiff peaks.

Prepare dessert topping following package directions. Fold egg whites gently into gelatin mixture; fold in ¾ *cup* whipped topping. (Refrigerate remaining topping.) If necessary, chill till gelatin mixture mounds. Pile atop first layer in crust. Chill till firm. Stir milk into remaining topping till smooth and fluffy; spoon around edge of pie. Makes 8 servings.

COCONUT-RASPBERRY DESSERTS
119 calories/serving

The jiffy topping, served over fresh berries and sherbet, contains bits of toasted coconut—

> 1 envelope from a 2½-ounce package low-calorie dessert topping mix
> ¼ cup shredded coconut, toasted
> 1 pint raspberry sherbet
> 1 cup fresh raspberries

Prepare topping mix following package directions. Fold in coconut. Cover and chill. At serving time, stir sherbet just to soften; spoon into 8 small sherbet dishes. Reserve a few berries for garnish; spoon remainder over sherbet. Top with whipped topping. Garnish with berries. Serve at once. Makes 8 servings.

For layer upon layer of strawberry flavor, prepare delectable Strawberry Ribbon Pie. The fluffy filling, made with fresh strawberries, sits atop a crimson gelatin layer and a graham cracker crust.

GRAPEFRUIT SPARKLE
86 calories/serving

Candied orange peel adds an interesting topper to wine-sauced pink and white grapefruit—

> 3 medium pink grapefruit
> 3 medium white grapefruit
> ¼ cup dry red wine
> 1 cup low-calorie lemon-lime
>   carbonated beverage, chilled
> 2 tablespoons slivered candied orange
>   peel

Section grapefruit into bowl, catching juices. Sprinkle wine over grapefruit. Chill several hours or overnight. At serving time, spoon grapefruit and juice into serving dishes. Slowly pour some carbonated beverage over each serving. Garnish fruit with orange peel. Serve immediately. Makes 8 servings.

PEACHES-AND-CREAM PARFAITS
127 calories/serving

Delicately flavored with cardamom—

> ½ cup low-calorie imitation sour cream
>   or ½ cup yogurt mixed with
>   2 teaspoons sugar
> ½ cup cream-style cottage cheese
> 2 tablespoons sugar
> ⅛ teaspoon ground cardamom
>   Few drops almond extract
>   Few drops lemon extract
> 4 fresh medium peaches

In blender container combine all ingredients *except* peaches. Cover; blend till smooth. If desired, chill several hours. At serving time peel, pit, and slice peaches. Alternate sauce and peach slices in 4 parfait glasses. Serve immediately. Makes 4 servings.

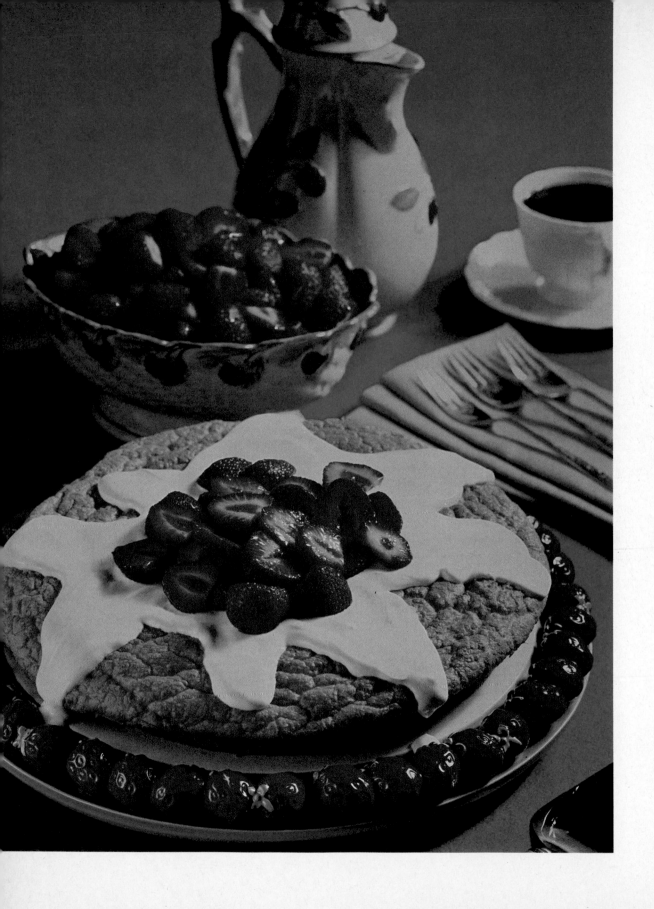

MOCHA SOUFFLE
107 calories/serving

¼ cup all-purpose flour
¼ cup sugar
3 tablespoons unsweetened cocoa
    powder
2 teaspoons instant coffee powder
¼ teaspoon salt
1 cup buttermilk
4 eggs, separated
1 teaspoon vanilla
2 tablespoons sugar

Combine first 5 ingredients in saucepan. Stir in milk. Cook and stir till thickened and bubbly; remove from heat. Cool. Beat egg yolks till thick and lemon-colored. Slowly blend into mocha mixture. Beat egg whites and vanilla till soft peaks form. Gradually add remaining sugar, beating to stiff peaks. Fold a little beaten egg whites into mocha mixture; gently fold mocha mixture into whites. Turn into *ungreased* 6-cup soufflé dish. Bake at 300° for 55 to 60 minutes. Serves 8.

BAKED PUMPKIN CHEESECAKE
113 calories/serving

Combine ½ cup vanilla wafer crumbs and 1 tablespoon melted butter or margarine; press into bottom of 8-inch springform pan. Bake at 325° for 8 to 10 minutes; cool. Press 2 cups dry cottage cheese through sieve; beat in 3 egg yolks, 1 cup canned pumpkin, ¼ cup reconstituted nonfat dry milk, ½ cup sugar, 1 teaspoon vanilla, ½ teaspoon ground cinnamon, ¼ teaspoon ground ginger, and ¼ teaspoon ground nutmeg till smooth. Fold in 3 stiffly beaten egg whites. Spoon into crust. Bake at 325° till set, 25 minutes. Chill. Garnish with ground nutmeg. if desired. Serves 12.

Special company fare

← *You won't believe that Sweet Strawberry Omelet is a low-calorie dessert when you taste the golden omelet with its smooth topper and fresh berries.*

SWEET STRAWBERRY OMELET
98 calories/serving

4 eggs, separated
½ cup yogurt
2 tablespoons sugar
1 tablespoon butter or margarine
¼ cup frozen whipped dessert
    topping, thawed
3 tablespoons skim milk
2 teaspoons sugar
2 cups fresh strawberries, sliced

Beat egg whites till frothy; add 2 tablespoons water and ¼ teaspoon salt. Beat to stiff peaks. Beat egg yolks till thick and lemon-colored; beat in ¼ *cup* yogurt and 2 tablespoons sugar. Fold yolks into whites. Melt butter in 10-inch ovenproof skillet; heat till drop of water sizzles. Pour in eggs; spread to edges. Reduce heat; cook 8 minutes. Finish cooking in oven at 325° till knife comes out clean, 10 to 12 minutes. Loosen omelet; slide onto warm platter. Combine remaining yogurt, topping, milk, and sugar; spoon over omelet. Top with a few berries. Pass remaining. Serves 8.

DANISH CONES WITH APRICOT
103 calories/serving

¼ cup butter or margarine, melted
⅓ cup sugar
2 eggs
½ cup sifted all-purpose flour
1 8-ounce can apricot halves (juice
    pack), drained and chopped
1 2-ounce package regular dessert
    topping mix
1 tablespoon brandy

Combine butter and sugar; beat in eggs, then flour. Drop two 1-tablespoon dollops batter 4 inches apart on well-greased baking sheet. Spread to 3-inch circles. Bake at 400° for 4 or 5 minutes. Remove from sheet; roll into cones. Cool. Repeat with remaining batter.

Using water in place of milk, prepare topping following package directions. Fold in apricots and brandy. Spoon into cones; top with ground nutmeg, if desired. Serves 15.

ORANGY BAVARIAN CREAM
102 calories/serving

   2 envelopes unflavored gelatin
   ⅓ cup sugar
   Dash salt
   **1 10½-ounce can mandarin orange
      sections (water pack)**
   **1 6-ounce can frozen orange juice
      concentrate, thawed**
   **1 cup frozen whipped dessert topping,
      thawed**

In saucepan combine gelatin, sugar, and salt. Drain oranges, reserving juice. Cut up oranges and set aside. Add water to juice to make 1 cup; stir into gelatin mixture. Stir over low heat till gelatin dissolves. Stir in 1¼ cups cold water and juice concentrate. Chill till partially set. Whip gelatin mixture till light and fluffy. Fold in dessert topping and oranges. Turn into 6½-cup mold. Chill till firm, 4 to 5 hours or overnight. Makes 10 servings.

APRICOT SPANISH CREAM
101 calories/serving with sugar
 69 calories/serving with noncaloric sweetener

Apricot halves may be pureed for a sauce—

   **1 16-ounce can apricot halves
      (water pack)**
   1 envelope unflavored gelatin
   **¼ cup sugar or noncaloric sweetener
      to equal ¼ cup sugar**
   Dash salt
   1 cup reconstituted nonfat dry milk
   2 beaten egg yolks
   2 egg whites

Drain apricot halves, reserving liquid. In saucepan combine gelatin, sugar or noncaloric sweetener, salt, reserved apricot liquid, milk, and beaten egg yolks. Stir over low heat till gelatin and sugar dissolve. Remove from heat; chill till partially set.
   Beat egg whites till stiff peaks form. Fold into gelatin mixture. Turn into six 6-ounce custard cups. Chill till firm. Unmold; top with apricot halves. Makes 6 servings.

BLUEBERRY CUSTARD MOUSSE
94 calories/serving

A creamy, rich molded dessert flecked with luscious, fresh blueberries—

   1 envelope unflavored gelatin
   **1 3¼-ounce package regular vanilla
      pudding mix**
   1½ cups reconstituted nonfat dry milk
   1 tablespoon lemon juice
      • • •
   2 egg whites
   **1 cup whipped low-calorie dessert
      topping**
   1 cup fresh blueberries
   **¼ cup whipped low-calorie dessert
      topping**

In saucepan combine unflavored gelatin, vanilla pudding mix, and reconstituted nonfat dry milk. Bring mixture to boiling, stirring constantly. Remove from heat and stir in lemon juice. Cover surface of pudding with waxed paper; chill thoroughly. Stir till smooth.
   Beat egg whites till stiff peaks form. Fold into pudding mixture. Fold in the 1 cup whipped topping and fresh blueberries. Turn into 4½-cup mold. Chill, covered, till mixture is firm, 3 to 4 hours or overnight. To serve, unmold onto plate. Garnish with the ¼ cup whipped topping. Makes 8 servings.

LOW-CALORIE COOKING TIP

Preparing a little caramelized sugar turns baked custard into gourmet fare, yet keeps it within calorie limits. After the sugar is melted and golden brown, pour into dish; rotate to coat bottom.

For dessert, there's nothing quite like Baked Caramel Custard topped with shimmery, golden, caramelized sugar. To set off this dessert, serve it in your prettiest stemmed glassware. Your family and your guests will love it.

BAKED CARAMEL CUSTARD
121 calories/serving

- 2 cups reconstituted nonfat dry milk
- 2 beaten eggs
- 2 beaten egg yolks
- ¼ cup sugar
- ½ teaspoon vanilla
- 2 tablespoons sugar

Scald milk and cool slightly. Combine whole eggs, egg yolks, and ¼ cup sugar; slowly stir in scalded milk. Add vanilla and set aside.

In a small heavy skillet stir 2 tablespoons sugar over low heat till melted and golden brown; remove from heat. Pour melted sugar into 1-quart casserole and rotate casserole to coat bottom with syrup. Pour custard mixture into casserole. Set in shallow pan on oven rack; pour hot water around casserole 1 inch deep. Bake at 325° till knife inserted off-center comes out clean, 1 hour and 15 minutes. (Custard will be soft.) Chill thoroughly. Unmold to serve. Makes 6 servings.

ORANGE PUDDING CAKE
118 calories/serving

- 3 egg whites
- ¼ cup sugar
- 3 egg yolks
- 1 teaspoon grated orange peel
- ¼ cup orange juice
- 2 tablespoons butter or margarine, melted
- ¼ cup sifted all-purpose flour
- ¼ cup sugar
- 1½ cups reconstituted nonfat dry milk

Beat egg whites with dash salt till soft peaks form. Gradually add first ¼ cup sugar, beating to stiff peaks. Beat egg yolks with orange peel, juice, and butter. Combine flour and remaining sugar. Stir into egg yolk mixture along with milk. Fold in egg whites. Pour batter into 8x8x2-inch baking pan. Place in larger pan on oven rack. Pour hot water into larger pan 1 inch deep. Bake at 350° for 35 to 40 minutes. Serve warm or chilled. Serves 9.

CHERRY CREPES
143 calories/serving

⅓ cup sifted all-purpose flour
1 tablespoon sugar
¾ cup reconstituted nonfat dry milk
1 whole egg
1 egg yolk
Dash salt

• • •

½ cup low-calorie imitation sour cream
    or ½ cup yogurt mixed with 2
    teaspoons sugar
1 tablespoon sugar
⅛ teaspoon ground cinnamon

• • •

1 tablespoon cornstarch
¼ cup sugar
1 teaspoon grated orange peel
1 cup low-calorie cranberry juice
    cocktail
1 20-ounce can pitted tart red cherries,
    drained
Few drops red food coloring

Combine flour, 1 tablespoon sugar, milk, egg, egg yolk, and salt; beat till smooth. *Lightly* grease a 6-inch skillet; heat. Remove from heat; spoon in about 2 tablespoons batter. Rotate pan so batter is spread evenly over bottom. Return to heat; brown on one side only. To remove, invert pan onto paper toweling. Repeat with remaining batter.

Combine imitation sour cream, 1 tablespoon sugar, and cinnamon. Spread unbrowned side of crepes with mixture. Roll up crepes. Combine cornstarch and ¼ cup sugar; stir cornstarch mixture and orange peel into cranberry juice cocktail. Stir in cherries and few drops red food coloring. Cook and stir till thickened and bubbly. Place crepes in blazer pan of chafing dish; pour cherry sauce over crepes. Heat through. Makes 8 servings.

Spectacular company finale

← *Your guests are sure to enjoy cinnamon cream-filled Cherry Crepes, a low-calorie specialty served with a bright red cranberry-cherry sauce.*

CRANBERRY-APRICOT WAFFLES
127 calories/serving

½ cup sifted all-purpose flour
½ teaspoon baking powder
¼ teaspoon salt
4 egg yolks
1 cup cream-style cottage cheese
1 tablespoon butter or margarine, melted
4 stiffly beaten egg whites
1 16-ounce can apricot halves
    (juice pack)
3 tablespoons sugar
2 tablespoons cornstarch
1 cup low-calorie cranberry juice
    cocktail
¼ teaspoon almond extract
6 drops red food coloring

Sift together flour, baking powder, and salt. In blender combine yolks, cottage cheese, butter, and flour mixture. Blend till smooth. Fold whites into batter. Bake in preheated waffle baker. Drain and cut up apricots, reserving juice. In saucepan combine sugar and cornstarch; stir in apricot juice and cranberry juice. Cook and stir till thick and bubbly. Stir in extract, food coloring, and apricots. Serve warm over waffles. Makes 10 servings.

PINEAPPLE-ANGEL DELIGHT
137 calories/serving

1 20-ounce can crushed pineapple
    (juice pack)
1 tablespoon cornstarch
1¾ cups reconstituted nonfat dry milk
1 4-serving envelope low-calorie
    vanilla pudding mix
½ cup lemon-flavored yogurt
5 cups ½-inch angel cake cubes

Drain pineapple, reserving juice. In saucepan blend reserved juice into cornstarch. Cook and stir till thickened and bubbly; set aside. Using 1¾ cups reconstituted milk, prepare pudding mix following package directions. Stir in thickened pineapple juice, drained pineapple, yogurt, and cake cubes. Spread in 9x9x2-inch pan. Chill 4 or 5 hours. Serves 9.

RASPBERRY BAVARIAN CAKE
128 calories/serving

> 1 package angel cake mix
> ½ cup evaporated skim milk
> 1 10-ounce package frozen raspberries, thawed
> 1 envelope unflavored gelatin
>   Red food coloring

Prepare angel cake following package directions; cool. Cut cake crosswise into 3 layers. Pour evaporated milk into shallow container; freeze till ice crystals form around edges. Drain raspberries, reserving syrup. Add water to syrup to make 1 cup. In saucepan soften gelatin in ¼ cup cold water; stir over low heat till gelatin dissolves. Stir in reserved raspberry syrup. Cool. Cut up raspberries.

In chilled bowl beat gelatin and milk to stiff peaks. Tint pink with food coloring. Fold in berries. Spread 1¼ cups berry mixture between layers. Spread sides and top with remaining mixture. Chill briefly. Serves 16.

A delicate, light raspberry mixture doubles as the flavorful filling and frosting for this attractive, triple-layered Raspberry Bavarian Cake.

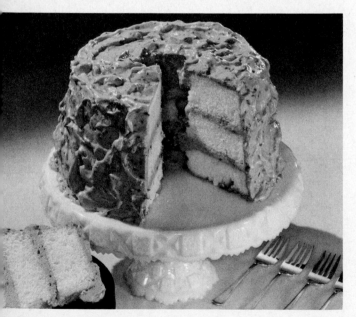

LEMONADE ROLL
133 calories/serving

> ¾ cup sifted all-purpose flour
> 1 teaspoon baking powder
> 4 egg yolks
> ¼ cup granulated sugar
> 1 6-ounce can frozen lemonade concentrate, thawed
> 4 egg whites
> 2 tablespoons granulated sugar
> 1 tablespoon sifted powdered sugar
>   Reconstituted nonfat dry milk
> 1 3½-ounce package vanilla whipped dessert mix

Sift together flour, baking powder, and ½ teaspoon salt. Beat egg yolks till thick and lemon-colored. Gradually beat in ¼ cup sugar till light. Beat in ½ *cup* concentrate alternately with flour mixture. Beat egg whites to soft peaks; gradually add 2 tablespoons sugar, beating to stiff peaks. Fold in lemon-egg mixture. Spread batter in waxed paper-lined 15½x10½x1-inch jelly-roll pan. Bake at 375° for 12 to 15 minutes. Loosen sides and turn onto towel sprinkled with powdered sugar. Remove paper. Starting at narrow end, roll cake and towel together; cool thoroughly.

Using remaining concentrate plus milk to make 1 cup, prepare dessert mix following package directions. Unroll cake; spread with filling and reroll. Chill 1 hour. Serves 12.

CRÈME DE MENTHE CREAM PUFFS
122 calories/serving

> 1 envelope unflavored gelatin
> 3 tablespoons green crème de menthe
> 1 envelope from a 2½-ounce package low-calorie dessert topping mix
>   Cream Puffs (page 24)

Soften gelatin in ¾ cup cold water. Heat and stir till gelatin dissolves. Stir in crème de menthe. Cool. Prepare topping mix according to package directions. Fold crème de menthe mixture into topping. Chill till mixture mounds, about 30 minutes; stir often. Spoon mixture into Cream Puffs. Makes 8 servings.

PEACH-ANGEL FLUFF
74 calories/serving

In saucepan combine ¼ cup sugar, 2 envelopes unflavored gelatin, and ¼ teaspoon salt; add 1 cup cold water. Stir over low heat till gelatin dissolves. Chill till partially set. Peel and pit 6 fresh medium peaches. Reserve one peach half; dip in ascorbic acid color keeper *or* lemon juice mixed with water. Dice remaining peaches; add 2 tablespoons lemon juice and 4 or 5 drops almond extract.

Place gelatin mixture, 4 egg whites, and *half* the diced peaches in large bowl. Beat with electric mixer till fluffy, about 10 minutes. Chill till partially set. Prepare 1 envelope from a 2½-ounce package low-calorie dessert topping mix following package directions. Fold remaining diced peaches and whipped topping into partially set gelatin. Line sides of 8-inch springform pan with 8 ladyfingers, split lengthwise; pour in filling. Chill till firm. Remove sides of pan. Slice reserved peach half; garnish top with peaches. Makes 16 servings.

The fresh flavor of juicy peaches mixed into a fluffy filling and surrounded by ladyfinger halves makes decorative Peach-Angel Fluff a perfect party-goer.

CHERRY-RHUBARB PIE
149 calories/serving

> 1 20-ounce can pitted tart red cherries
> 1 tablespoon orange juice
> 3 tablespoons all-purpose flour
>   Noncaloric sweetener to equal
>   ¾ cup sugar
> 1 teaspoon almond extract
>   Few drops red food coloring
> 4 cups rhubarb cut in 1-inch pieces
> 1 unbaked 9-inch Cottage Cheese
>   Pastry shell (page 43)
> 2 zwieback, crushed
> 1 teaspoon grated orange peel

Drain cherries, reserving ½ cup juice. Combine orange juice, flour, and dash salt; stir in cherry juice, sweetener, and ½ cup water. Cook and stir till bubbly; cook 1 minute. Stir in extract and food coloring. Combine cherries, rhubarb, and juice mixture. Pour into pastry shell. Cover with foil. Bake at 400° for 40 minutes. Toss zwieback and peel; sprinkle over pie. Bake 5 to 10 minutes more. Serves 8.

CRANBERRY TEA BREAD
111 calories/serving

No spread or topping is needed—

> 1½ cups sifted all-purpose flour
> ¾ cup sugar
> 1 teaspoon baking powder
> ½ teaspoon baking soda
> ½ teaspoon salt
> 3 tablespoons shortening
> 1 teaspoon grated orange peel
> ¾ cup orange juice
> 1 beaten egg
> 1 cup fresh cranberries, coarsely
>   chopped

Sift together flour, sugar, baking powder, and salt. Cut in shortening. Combine orange peel, orange juice, and egg. Add to dry ingredients, mixing just to moisten. Fold in berries. Turn into greased 8½x4½x2⅝-inch loaf pan. Bake at 350° for 50 to 55 minutes. Cool. Wrap and store overnight. Makes 16 servings.

Holiday Features

PUMPKIN TORTE

116 calories/serving

1 envelope unflavored gelatin
¼ cup sugar
Dash salt
½ cup cold water
1½ cups canned pumpkin
1 teaspoon pumpkin pie spice
1 envelope from a 2½-ounce package
low-calorie dessert topping mix
20 gingersnaps (2¼ inch diameter)

In small saucepan combine gelatin, sugar, and salt; add water. Stir over low heat till gelatin dissolves. Stir in pumpkin and pumpkin pie spice; chill till partially set.

Prepare topping mix following package directions; fold into pumpkin mixture. Spread 1 tablespoon pumpkin mixture on each cookie. Stack 4 or 5 together; chill 15 minutes. On serving plate, stand stacks on edge, making 1 long roll. Frost with remaining pumpkin mixture. Refrigerate several hours or overnight. Garnish with 1 gingersnap, crushed, if desired. To serve, slice diagonally. Makes 10 servings.

THREE-FRUIT COMPOTE

132 calories/serving

An idea for New Year's Eve—

Thaw two 10-ounce packages frozen raspberries. Drain, reserving liquid. Drain two 16-ounce cans apricot halves (water pack), reserving liquid. Combine fruit liquids and add water, if necessary, to make 3 cups. In saucepan blend 4 teaspoons cornstarch and dash salt. Stir in liquid. Cook and stir till mixture thickens and bubbles. Remove from heat.

Add raspberries, apricots, and two 16-ounce cans purple plums (water pack), drained. Chill. Serve in large glass bowl. Top with 1 cup low-calorie imitation sour cream *or* 1 cup yogurt mixed with 2 teaspoons sugar. Serves 12.

PEPPERMINT MERINGUES

84 calories/serving

Petite heart-shaped meringues are perfect to serve at a Valentine's Day party—

Individual Meringue Shells (page 52)
1 4-serving envelope low-calorie vanilla
pudding mix
1 3-ounce package Neufchâtel cheese
¼ teaspoon peppermint extract
2 tablespoons sugar
2 egg whites
8 maraschino cherries, halved

Prepare *double* recipe of Individual Meringue Shells, *except* shape as follows: cut heart pattern from a 3½-inch square of paper. Cover two baking sheets with plain brown paper. Draw 8 hearts from pattern on each sheet. Spread meringue over each heart shape, making ¼-inch layer. With pastry tube, pipe on rims about ¾ inch high. Bake as directed.

Prepare pudding mix according to package directions. Remove from heat. Cut Neufchâtel cheese in pieces and add to hot pudding. Beat till cheese melts. Let mixture cool about 10 minutes. Stir in peppermint extract. Chill well. Gradually adding sugar, beat egg whites till soft peaks form. Fold egg whites into pudding mixture. Chill thoroughly. Just before serving, spoon pudding mixture into heart-shaped meringue shells. Top each serving with a maraschino cherry half. Makes 16 servings.

(*Or,* to make 8 meringues, prepare 1 recipe heart-shaped Individual Meringue Shells. Fill with *half* the pudding mixture. Chill remaining pudding to serve another time.)

A Thanksgiving dessert

Accent your roast turkey dinner by serving slices of spicy Pumpkin Torte, a dessert made by spreading a pumpkin mixture between gingersnaps.

CHRISTMAS CONFETTI SQUARES
132 calories/serving

Snowy white squares dotted with red and green—

- 3 **envelopes unflavored gelatin**
- 2 **cups low-calorie cranberry juice cocktail**
- 3 **tablespoons sugar**
- 1 **4-serving envelope low-calorie lime-flavored gelatin**
- 2 **cups boiling water**
- 3 **cups unsweetened pineapple juice**
- 1 **envelope from a 2½-ounce package low-calorie dessert topping mix**
- 12 **vanilla wafers, crushed**

Soften *1 envelope* gelatin in cranberry juice. Add *1 tablespoon* sugar. Stir over low heat till dissolved. Pour into an 8x8x2-inch or 9x5x3-inch pan; chill till firm. Dissolve lime gelatin in boiling water. Pour into another 8x8x2-inch or 9x5x3-inch pan; chill till firm.

Soften remaining unflavored gelatin in pineapple juice. Add remaining 2 tablespoons sugar. Dissolve over low heat. Chill till partially set. Prepare topping following package directions; fold into pineapple gelatin. Cut cranberry and lime gelatin into ½-inch cubes. Reserve 1 cup cubes. Fold remaining cubes into topping mixture. Sprinkle wafer crumbs in bottom of 8x8x2-inch pan. Pour filling over. Chill till firm. Top with reserved cubes. Serves 9.

If you serve crispy Santa's Whiskers and fluffy Eggnog, you can forget the calories and still enjoy the holiday refreshments. Two of these mouth-watering cookies served along with the beverage totals only 123 calories.

STEAMED CRANBERRY PUDDING
122 calories/serving

An ideal meal-ending for a Thanksgiving or Christmas dinner—

- 1 cup sifted all-purpose flour
- 1 teaspoon baking soda
- ¼ teaspoon ground cinnamon
- ¼ teaspoon ground cloves
- ¼ teaspoon ground nutmeg
- ⅓ cup hot water
- ⅓ cup light molasses
- ¼ cup brown sugar
- 1 cup halved fresh cranberries
- ½ cup whipped low-calorie dessert topping

Sift together all-purpose flour, baking soda, ground cinnamon, ground cloves, and ground nutmeg. Combine hot water, light molasses, and brown sugar; stir into flour mixture along with halved fresh cranberries. Pour batter into greased 1-quart mold. Cover with greased foil; tie securely with string.

Place mold on rack in deep kettle; add boiling water to kettle, 1 inch deep. Cover; steam for 2½ hours, adding more boiling water to kettle, if needed. Cool steamed pudding 10 minutes; unmold. Serve warm with whipped low-calorie dessert topping. Makes 8 servings.

Dessert toppings vary in calories

If you're planning to have a dollop of whipped topping on your favorite dessert, remember that toppings differ in calorie count. One tablespoon whipped cream contains 28 calories, while the same amount of frozen whipped dessert topping has 16. Regular whipped topping from a mix counts 14 calories per tablespoon compared to 7 calories for the same amount of whipped low-calorie dessert topping from a mix.

SANTA'S WHISKERS
39 calories/cookie

Get their name from the coconut 'whiskers'—

- ½ cup butter or margarine
- ¾ cup sugar
- 1 teaspoon vanilla
- 3 tablespoons skim milk
- 1½ cups sifted all-purpose flour
- ½ teaspoon baking powder
- ½ teaspoon salt
- ¾ cup coarsely chopped fresh cranberries
- ½ cup shredded coconut

Cream butter or margarine, sugar, and vanilla till light and fluffy; beat in skim milk. Sift together flour, baking powder, and salt; mix into creamed mixture. Stir in chopped cranberries. Form dough into 2 rolls, each about 8 inches long. (Dough will be very soft.) Roll in shredded coconut. Wrap; chill several hours or overnight. Slice thin. Bake on ungreased cookie sheet at 375° till edges are golden, 12 to 15 minutes. Makes 5 dozen cookies.

EGGNOG
45 calories/serving

Spiked with brandy or rum flavoring—

- 4 egg yolks
  Noncaloric sweetener to equal ⅓ cup sugar
- ¼ teaspoon salt
- 4 cups reconstituted nonfat dry milk
  • • •
- 1 teaspoon vanilla
- ½ teaspoon brandy or rum flavoring
- 4 egg whites
  Ground nutmeg

Beat egg yolks with sweetener. Add salt; stir in milk. Cook over medium heat, stirring constantly, till mixture lightly coats a metal spoon. Add flavorings. Cool. Beat egg whites to soft peaks. Carefully fold custard into egg whites. Chill 3 or 4 hours. To serve, sprinkle with ground nutmeg. Makes 14 (½-cup) servings.

low-calorie dessert
SPECIALTIES

Streamlined desserts can fulfill duties other than just controlling calories. Minute-minded recipes like Orangy Date-Nut Rounds and spiced Apricot-Pineapple Kuchen speed meal preparation; diabetic desserts suit a special dieter's needs; and small-sized desserts reward the lone calorie counter.

Minute-Ready Desserts

FRUIT-FILLED ORANGES
98 calories/serving

Orange cups hold a honey-glazed mixture of oranges, pineapple, strawberries, and dates—

> 3-medium oranges
> 1 8-ounce can pineapple tidbits
>   (juice pack)
> ½ cup fresh strawberries, sliced
> ¼ cup snipped pitted dates
> 1 tablespoon honey
> 2 teaspoons lemon juice

Cut oranges in half. Hollow out halves; reserve shells. Cut away excess white membrane from orange pulp; cut up fruit, reserving juice. Drain pineapple tidbits, reserving juice. Combine cut-up oranges, pineapple, strawberries, and dates. Add enough reserved pineapple juice to reserved orange juice to make ⅓ cup; combine with honey and lemon juice. Pour over fruit. Chill well. To serve, fill orange shells with fruit mixture. Makes 6 servings.

SPECIAL SPICED APRICOTS
50 calories/serving

Brandy flavoring is the special touch—

> 1 16-ounce can apricot halves
>   (water pack)
> 2 tablespoons brown sugar
> 1 teaspoon lemon juice
> 6 inches stick cinnamon
> 1 teaspoon brandy flavoring

Drain apricot halves, reserving juice; set apricots aside. In small saucepan combine reserved apricot juice, brown sugar, lemon juice, and stick cinnamon. Simmer apricot juice mixture, uncovered, for 5 minutes. Add apricot halves; heat through. Cool. Stir in brandy flavoring. Chill thoroughly. Remove stick cinnamon before serving. Serves 5.

BLACKBERRY-SAUCED PEARS
126 calories/serving

> 1 3-ounce package Neufchâtel cheese,
>   softened
> 1 tablespoon skim milk
> 1 teaspoon sugar
> 3 fresh medium pears
>   Ascorbic acid color keeper or lemon
>   juice mixed with water
> ½ cup low-calorie blackberry jelly
> 2 tablespoons dry red wine

Mix first 3 ingredients till smooth and creamy. Peel, halve, and core pears; dip in color keeper. Place, cavity side up, in shallow baking pan. Using pastry tube, pipe some of cheese mixture into each pear cavity. Bake at 350° till pears are warm, about 15 minutes.

   In saucepan mix jelly, 2 tablespoons water, and wine; cook and stir till heated through. To serve, place one pear half in each serving dish; spoon sauce over. Makes 6 servings.

APRICOTS MELBA
92 calories/serving

> 8 fresh medium apricots, halved
>   and pitted
> ¾ cup raspberry sherbet
> ½ cup fresh red raspberries
>   Few drops almond extract

Place 4 apricot halves in each serving dish. Stir raspberry sherbet to soften; mix in fresh raspberries and almond extract. Spoon over apricots. Serve at once. Makes 4 servings.

Easy and elegant

No one will guess it took only minutes to prepare Blackberry-Sauced Pears. You make the jelly-based sauce while the cheese-filled pears bake. →

APRICOT-PINEAPPLE KUCHEN
123 calories/serving

Pictured on pages 68 and 69 —

>   1 package flaky-style refrigerated
>   biscuits (10 biscuits)
>   1 16-ounce can apricot halves (water
>   pack), drained and quartered
>   1 cup pineapple tidbits (juice pack),
>   drained
>   ¼ cup sugar
>   1 teaspoon grated lemon peel
>   ¼ teaspoon ground cinnamon
>   ¾ cup low-calorie imitation sour cream
>   or 1 cup yogurt mixed with
>   2 teaspoons sugar
>   1 beaten egg
>   2 tablespoons sugar

With fingers, flatten flaky-style refrigerated biscuits in 13x9x2-inch baking pan, sealing edges together. Build up edges around pan slightly. Bake at 350° for 5 minutes.

Combine quartered apricots, pineapple tidbits, ¼ cup sugar, grated lemon peel, and ground cinnamon; toss together lightly. Spoon mixture over partially baked biscuits.

Blend together imitation sour cream, egg, and 2 tablespoons sugar; drizzle over fruit. Bake at 350° for 20 minutes. Serves 12.

FRESH FRUIT AND WINE MEDLEY
94 calories/serving

Orange juice and port complement the fruit —

>   ⅓ cup port
>   ¼ cup orange juice
>   1 tablespoon lemon juice
>   2 tablespoons sugar
>   1 fresh medium peach, peeled and
>   sliced
>   1 cup fresh strawberries, sliced
>   1 medium banana, sliced
>   1 fresh medium pear, peeled and diced

Combine port, orange juice, lemon juice, and sugar. Mix fruits in bowl. Pour juice mixture over; toss. Chill thoroughly. Makes 6 servings.

PEACHY RASPBERRY FONDUE
141 calories/serving

>   1 10-ounce package frozen raspberries,
>   thawed
>   4 teaspoons cornstarch
>   1 3-ounce package Neufchâtel cheese,
>   softened
>   ¼ cup reconstituted nonfat dry milk
>   6 fresh medium peaches, peeled and
>   cut in cubes
>   Ascorbic acid color keeper or lemon
>   juice mixed with water

In saucepan crush undrained berries slightly. Blend cornstarch and ¼ cup cold water; add to berries. Cook and stir till thickened and bubbly. Sieve; discard seeds. Pour into fondue pot; place over fondue burner. Beat cheese with milk till smooth. Stir into sauce. Heat through. Dip peaches in color keeper. Spear peach cube with fondue fork; dip in fondue. Makes 6 servings.

ORANGY DATE-NUT ROUNDS
133 calories/serving

Pictured on pages 68 and 69 —

>   1 egg
>   2 tablespoons sugar
>   2 tablespoons skim milk
>   ½ teaspoon grated orange peel
>   ½ teaspoon grated lemon peel
>   1 tablespoon orange juice
>   1 teaspoon lemon juice
>   1 cup whipped low-calorie dessert
>   topping
>   6 ½-inch slices canned date-nut roll
>   6 orange slices
>   6 fresh strawberries, halved

In small saucepan beat egg, sugar, and milk. Cook and stir over low heat till slightly thickened, about 5 minutes. Stir in peels and fruit juices. Cool thoroughly. Fold in whipped topping. Chill. To serve, top date-nut slices with orange topping. Cut and twist orange slices; place one slice with 2 strawberry halves alongside each serving. Makes 6 servings.

It's easy to fill repeat requests for Strawberry-Yogurt Medley, a combination of juicy, fresh fruits, because the creamy smooth topper is simply strawberry yogurt, Neufchâtel cheese, and a small amount of sugar.

STRAWBERRY-YOGURT MEDLEY

134 calories/serving

Fresh fruit served with a flavored yogurt topper—

 1 3-ounce package Neufchâtel cheese, softened
 ⅔ cup strawberry-flavored yogurt
 2 teaspoons sugar
 • • •
 2 cups fresh strawberries, halved
 2 medium oranges, peeled and sectioned
 1 medium banana, bias-sliced

Beat Neufchâtel cheese; stir in strawberry yogurt and sugar. Chill. Combine strawberries, orange sections, and sliced banana; chill. At serving time, spoon fruit into compote; spoon yogurt mixture over. Makes 8 servings.

CALYPSO FRUIT PLATTER

67 calories/serving

 1 medium banana, sliced
 ½ cup fresh cranberries
 3 tablespoons skim milk
 ½ cup yogurt
 3 tablespoons sugar
 ¼ teaspoon ground ginger
 ½ medium cantaloupe, peeled and cubed
 2 fresh medium pears, cored and cubed
 2 medium apples, cored and cubed

Blend first 3 ingredients in blender container till finely chopped. (When necessary, stop blender; scrape down sides with spatula.) Turn into bowl; stir in yogurt, sugar, and ginger. Chill. To serve, arrange fruit on platter. Spear fruit; dip in sauce. Makes 8 servings.

CITRUS-BERRY PARFAITS
112 calories/serving

> 1 teaspoon unflavored gelatin
> 1 10-ounce package frozen raspberries, thawed
> 1 3¾-ounce package lemon whipped dessert mix
> 2 tablespoons lime juice
> ½ teaspoon grated lime peel
> 2 stiffly beaten egg whites
> 1 cup whipped low-calorie dessert topping

Soften gelatin in ½ cup cold water; stir over low heat till gelatin dissolves. Stir into raspberries; chill till partially set. Using water in place of milk, prepare dessert mix according to package directions. Stir in lime juice and peel. Fold in egg whites and topping. Chill till partially set. In parfait glasses alternate whipped mixture and berries. Chill. Trim with lime slices, if desired. Serves 8.

Citrus-Berry Parfaits are as easy to make as they are pretty. Just layer the lemon-lime whipped dessert mixture between red raspberries and chill.

CHOCO-MALLOW PARFAITS
147 calories/serving

> 2 cups reconstituted nonfat dry milk
> 1 4-serving envelope low-calorie chocolate pudding mix
> 1½ cups whipped low-calorie dessert topping
> 12 marshmallows, cut up
> ¼ cup flaked coconut

Using reconstituted nonfat dry milk, prepare pudding mix according to package directions. Cover surface with waxed paper; cool thoroughly. Fold whipped topping into pudding. Chill. Toss marshmallows with coconut. Divide *half* the pudding mixture among 6 parfait glasses. Spoon marshmallow mixture into parfaits; top with remaining pudding. Serves 6.

POLYNESIAN PARFAITS
84 calories/serving

> 1 cup yogurt
> 1 tablespoon sugar
> ⅛ teaspoon ground nutmeg
> 1 10½-ounce can mandarin orange sections (water pack), drained
> 1 8-ounce can pineapple tidbits (juice pack), drained

Combine yogurt, sugar, and nutmeg. Layer mixture with oranges and pineapple in small sherbet dishes. Chill at least 1 hour. Serves 4.

PEACH-A-BERRY COMPOTE
78 calories/serving

> 1 16-ounce can sliced peaches (water pack), drained
> 1 cup seedless green grapes, halved
> 2 cups fresh red raspberries
> ⅓ cup low-calorie peach preserves
> 3 tablespoons water
> ¼ teaspoon ground cardamom

In compote combine fruits. Mix together remaining ingredients; add to fruits, stirring just to blend. Chill. Makes 6 servings.

PUDDING-PEAR DESSERT
116 calories/serving

Garnished with ladyfinger sandwiches—

> 2½ cups reconstituted nonfat dry milk
> 1 4-serving envelope low-calorie
>   vanilla pudding mix
> ½ teaspoon rum flavoring
> • • •
> 6 ladyfingers
> 2 tablespoons low-calorie strawberry
>   or raspberry preserves
> 1 8-ounce can pear halves (water pack),
>   drained and cubed

Using reconstituted nonfat dry milk, prepare pudding mix according to package directions. Stir in rum flavoring. Cool till almost set. Halve ladyfingers lengthwise; spread cut surfaces with preserves. Close; cut each in half again lengthwise. Spoon *half* the pudding into 6 sherbet dishes; add cubed pears. Insert 2 ladyfinger sticks in each dish; fill with remaining pudding. Chill. Makes 6 servings.

BLUEBERRY COBBLER
147 calories/serving

One tablespoon low-calorie whipped topping adds only seven calories per serving—

> 2 cups fresh blueberries
> 2 tablespoons sugar
> ⅔ cup water
> • • •
> ½ cup sifted all-purpose flour
> 2 tablespoons sugar
> 1 teaspoon baking powder
> ¼ teaspoon salt
> ¼ cup reconstituted nonfat dry milk
>   Ground nutmeg

In saucepan combine blueberries, 2 tablespoons sugar, and water; bring to boiling. In small bowl sift together flour, 2 tablespoons sugar, baking powder, and salt. Stir in milk. Drop in 4 portions onto boiling fruit. Sprinkle lightly with nutmeg. Cover; cook over medium heat for 10 to 12 minutes. Makes 4 servings.

Make your own fruit yogurt

To save calories, flavor commercial plain yogurt yourself. Stir 2 tablespoons crushed fresh fruit such as strawberries and 1 tablespoon sugar into 2 cups plain yogurt. Strawberry yogurt prepared the above way counts 89 calories per ½ cup compared to 133 calories for commercial strawberry yogurt. You save 44 calories.

STRAWBERRY SATIN
100 calories/serving

> 1 cup low-calorie lemon-lime
>   carbonated beverage
> 1 3¾-ounce package strawberry
>   whipped dessert mix
> 1 cup fresh strawberries
> ½ cup low-calorie imitation sour cream
>   or ½ cup yogurt mixed with
>   1 teaspoon sugar

Using carbonated beverage in place of milk and water, prepare dessert mix following package directions. Mash ½ *cup* of the berries; slice remaining and set aside. Fold mashed berries into whipped dessert. Stir imitation sour cream till smooth; fold into whipped mixture along with sliced berries. Spoon into sherbet dishes. Chill. Serves 6.

BUTTERSCOTCH-BANANA DESSERT
137 calories/serving

Using 1¾ *cups reconstituted nonfat dry milk,* prepare one 4-ounce package *instant* butterscotch pudding mix following package directions; let stand 5 minutes. Stir in ½ cup low-calorie imitation sour cream *or* ½ cup yogurt mixed with 1 teaspoon sugar; chill. Divide 4 medium bananas, sliced, among 8 sherbet dishes; top with pudding. Serves 8.

Diabetic Desserts

APRICOT-PEACH PUDDING

Food exchanges/serving: 2 fruit
(Carbohydrate, 20.2 grams; protein, .7 gram;
   fat, .1 gram)
80 calories/serving

   3 tablespoons quick-cooking tapioca
   1 12-ounce can apricot nectar (1½ cups)
   2 tablespoons lemon juice
     Noncaloric sweetener to equal
       ¼ cup sugar
   3 large fresh peaches, peeled, pitted,
     and chopped
   1 teaspoon vanilla
   ⅛ teaspoon ground mace

In saucepan combine tapioca, nectar, ½ cup cold water, lemon juice, and sweetener; let stand 5 minutes. Cook and stir till mixture is bubbly. Add peaches; heat through. Stir in vanilla and mace. Pour into dishes. Serves 6.

A note to diabetics

A diabetic often works from six food exchange lists prescribed by his physician or dietician. By using these lists properly, the diabetic is assured of maintaining his health. At the same time, it enables him to eat interesting and varied meals.

On pages 76 through 81, you'll discover an inviting array of dessert recipes that the whole family (including the diabetic) can enjoy together. Check the food exchanges per serving that appear directly beneath the recipe title along with the carbohydrate-fat-protein content, and calorie count. Then, select those recipes that fit into your individual program.

LEMON CHIFFON PIE

Food exchanges/serving: ½ meat, 1 bread, 1 fat
(Carbohydrate, 10.2 grams; protein, 5.1 grams;
   fat, 8.1 grams)
134 calories/serving

   2 tablespoons cornstarch
   1½ teaspoons unflavored gelatin
   ¼ cup reconstituted nonfat dry milk
   1¼ cups water
     Noncaloric sweetener to equal
       ⅓ cup sugar
   4 beaten egg yolks
   ¼ teaspoon grated lemon peel
   ¼ cup lemon juice
   1 or 2 drops lemon extract
   4 egg whites
   ½ teaspoon vanilla
   ¼ teaspoon cream of tartar
   1 baked 9-inch Yogurt Pastry shell
     (page 43)

In medium saucepan combine cornstarch and unflavored gelatin; gradually blend in reconstituted nonfat dry milk. Add water and noncaloric sweetener. Cook and stir over medium heat till mixture is thickened and bubbly. Gradually stir a moderate amount of hot mixture into beaten egg yolks; return mixture to saucepan. Cook 2 minutes more over low heat. Remove from heat; stir in lemon peel, lemon juice, and lemon extract. Cool mixture slightly.

   Beat egg whites with vanilla and cream of tartar till stiff peaks form. Fold beaten egg white mixture into cooled lemon mixture. Carefully pile into baked and cooled 9-inch Yogurt Pastry shell. Chill till firm, several hours or more. Makes 8 servings.

A golden twosome

Grace each serving of delicate Orange Chiffon →
Soufflé (page 78) with a special orange-studded
sauce — a worthy companion for this elegant dessert.

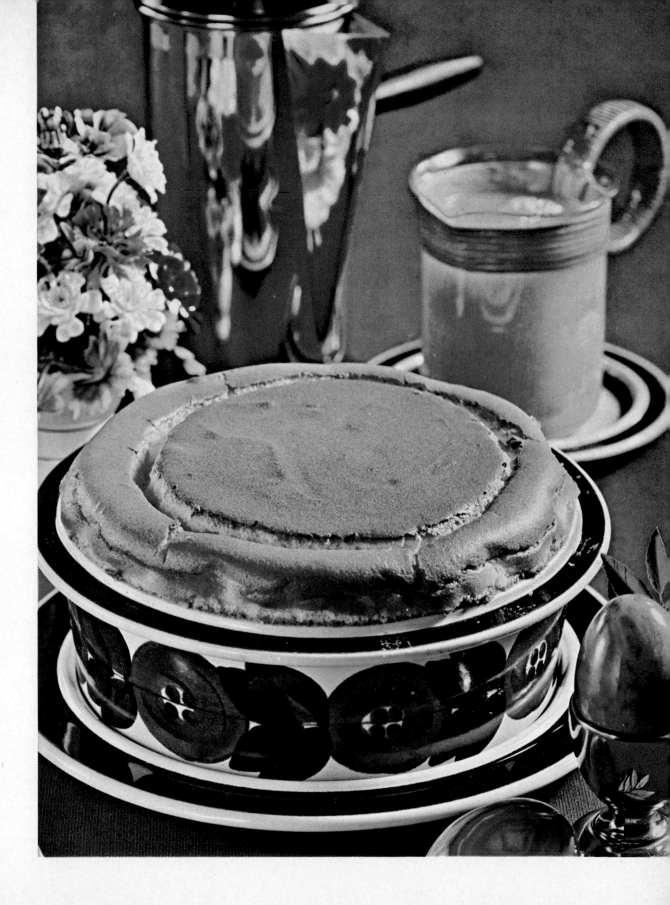

ORANGE CHIFFON SOUFFLÉ

Food exchanges/serving: ½ meat, ½ bread
(Carbohydrate, 6.7 grams; protein, 4.1 grams;
    fat, 4.0 grams)
80 calories/serving

Pictured on page 77 —

    1 tablespoon butter or margarine
    2 tablespoons cornstarch
      Dash salt
    ⅓ cup nonfat dry milk powder
    ¾ cup water
    1 teaspoon grated orange peel
    ½ cup orange juice
      Noncaloric sweetener to equal
        2 tablespoons sugar
    5 egg yolks
    5 egg whites
    4 teaspoons cornstarch
      Dash salt
      Noncaloric sweetener to equal
        2 tablespoons sugar
    1 medium orange
      Red and yellow food coloring

In saucepan melt butter or margarine; blend
in the 2 tablespoons cornstarch and dash salt.
Add nonfat dry milk powder and water all at
once. Cook quickly, stirring constantly, till
mixture is thickened and bubbly. Remove
from heat; stir in orange peel, orange juice,
and the noncaloric sweetener to equal 2 tablespoons sugar. Beat egg yolks till thick and
lemon-colored. Slowly add thickened orange
mixture to egg yolks, stirring constantly. Wash
beaters. Beat egg whites till stiff peaks form.
Carefully fold egg yolk mixture into beaten egg
whites. Gently pour mixture into an *ungreased*
2-quart soufflé dish with a foil collar.

  Bake at 325° till knife inserted off-center
comes out clean, about 70 minutes. Meanwhile, combine 4 teaspoons cornstarch, dash
salt, and remaining noncaloric sweetener in
small saucepan. Peel and dice orange, catching juice in bowl. Add water to juice to make
1 cup. Add orange juice to cornstarch mixture.
Cook and stir over low heat till mixture is
thickened and bubbly. Remove from heat; stir
in diced orange. Tint orange with food coloring. Serve warm with soufflé. Serves 10.

APPLESAUCE PIE

Food exchanges/serving: 2 B vegetable, ½ fruit,
    1½ fat
(Carbohydrate, 13.6 grams; protein, 4.4 grams;
    fat, 7.2 grams)
140 calories/serving

    1 16-ounce can applesauce (water pack)
    ½ cup buttermilk
    2 beaten eggs
      Noncaloric sweetener to equal
        ¼ cup sugar
    1 teaspoon lemon juice
    1 unbaked 8-inch Cottage Cheese
      Pastry shell (page 43)
      Ground cinnamon

Combine applesauce, buttermilk, beaten
eggs, noncaloric sweetener, and lemon juice;
mix well together. Pour mixture into unbaked
Cottage Cheese Pastry shell. Bake at 400° just
till firm in center, 50 to 55 minutes. Sprinkle
with ground cinnamon. Makes 8 servings.

BAKED BANANAS ESPECIALE

Food exchanges/serving: 2 B vegetable, 1 fat
(Carbohydrate, 13.7 grams; protein, 3.1 grams;
    fat, 4.9 grams)
128 calories/serving

UNDER **60** CALORIES

    2 firm medium bananas, sliced
    1 tablespoon water
    1 tablespoon lemon juice
    1 3-ounce package Neufchâtel cheese,
      softened
    2 tablespoons skim milk
    2 tablespoons low-calorie apricot
      preserves (artificially sweetened)
    ¼ teaspoon ground cinnamon
    1 tablespoon low-calorie apricot
      preserves (artificially sweetened)

Divide banana slices among four 6-ounce
custard cups. Brush bananas with mixture of
water and lemon juice. Whip cheese with milk
till fluffy; beat in the 2 tablespoons preserves
and cinnamon. Spoon cheese mixture over
bananas. Bake at 375° for 8 to 10 minutes.
Spoon remaining preserves atop cheese mixture. Bake 3 to 5 minutes more. Serves 4.

CHOCO-PEAR DESSERT

Food exchanges/serving: 2½ B vegetable
(Carbohydrate, 17.2 grams; protein, 3.4 grams;
   fat, .3 gram)
82 calories/serving

   2 cups reconstituted nonfat dry milk
   1 4-serving envelope low-calorie
      chocolate pudding mix
   1 16-ounce can pear halves (juice pack)
      Dash ground cinnamon

Using the 2 cups reconstituted nonfat dry milk,
prepare low-calorie pudding mix following
package directions. Cover surface of pudding
with waxed paper and chill. At serving time,
drain pears; place 1 pear half in each serving
dish. Sprinkle each pear half with cinnamon.
Top with pudding. Makes 6 servings.

CRANBERRY-ORANGE FLUFF

Food exchanges/serving: ½ fruit
(Carbohydrate, 5.1 grams; protein, 2.0 grams;
   fat, .1 gram)
29 calories/serving

   1 cup fresh cranberries
   1½ cups low-calorie cranberry
      juice cocktail
   1 envelope unflavored gelatin
   ¼ cup orange juice
   2 egg whites
      Noncaloric sweetener to equal
      2 tablespoons sugar

UNDER **60** *CALORIES*

In saucepan combine cranberries and cranberry juice cocktail. Bring to boiling; simmer
till skins pop, about 5 minutes. Meanwhile,
soften unflavored gelatin in orange juice. Stir
into cranberry mixture; heat and stir till gelatin dissolves. Press cranberry mixture through
sieve. Chill till partially set.
   Add unbeaten egg whites and noncaloric
sweetener to partially set gelatin mixture. Beat
with electric mixer till mixture is light, fluffy,
and double in volume, about 2 minutes. Chill
again, if necessary, till mixture mounds when
spooned. Pour into eight ½-cup molds. Chill
till firm. To serve, unmold in individual dessert dishes. Makes 8 servings.

BERRY-BUTTERMILK BAVARIAN

Food exchanges/serving: 1 meat, ¾ fruit
(Carbohydrate, 7.5 grams; protein, 6.7 grams;
   fat, 3.6 grams)
89 calories/serving

   1 envelope unflavored gelatin
   1¾ cups buttermilk
   2 beaten eggs
      Noncaloric sweetener to equal
      ⅓ cup sugar
   1 cup whipped low-calorie dessert
      topping
   1 cup fresh raspberries

In medium saucepan combine gelatin and buttermilk; let stand 5 minutes to soften. Add
beaten eggs and noncaloric sweetener. Cook
and stir over low heat till mixture coats a metal
spoon. Chill till partially set. Fold partially set
gelatin into whipped topping along with raspberries. Pour mixture into 4½-cup mold. Chill
till firm. Makes 6 servings.

BUTTERSCOTCH-RICE MOLD

Food exchanges/serving: 1 bread
(Carbohydrate, 15.0 grams; protein, 5.6 grams;
   fat, .1 gram)
94 calories/serving

   1 4-serving envelope low-calorie
      butterscotch pudding mix
   ¼ teaspoon salt
   ⅛ teaspoon ground cinnamon
   3½ cups reconstituted nonfat dry milk
   ½ cup uncooked packaged
      precooked rice
         • • •
   1 envelope unflavored gelatin
   ¼ cup cold water

In medium saucepan combine low-calorie
pudding mix, salt, and cinnamon. Gradually
blend in reconstituted nonfat dry milk. Add
uncooked rice. Cook and stir over medium
heat till mixture comes to boiling; simmer 2
minutes more. Meanwhile, soften unflavored
gelatin in cold water; add to pudding mixture.
Cook and stir till gelatin dissolves. Turn into
4½-cup mold. Chill till firm. Makes 7 servings.

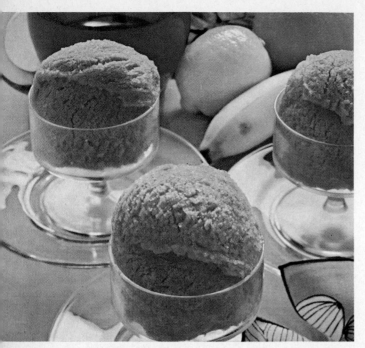

Four-Fruit Ice, a dessert that features cranberry, banana, orange, and lemon, is a pleasing treat for both diabetics and nondiabetics.

CHOCOLATE ICE CREAM

Food exchanges/serving: ½ meat, ½ milk, ½ fat
(Carbohydrate, 11.2 grams; protein, 8.6 grams;
  fat, 6.1 grams)
122 calories/serving

In saucepan combine 2 beaten eggs, one 14½-ounce can evaporated skim milk, 3 tablespoons unsweetened cocoa powder, dash salt, and noncaloric sweetener to equal ⅓ cup sugar. Cook and stir over low heat till mixture coats a metal spoon. Remove from heat; stir in 1 teaspoon vanilla. Cool.

Prepare 1 envelope from a 2½-ounce package low-calorie dessert topping mix following package directions; fold into chocolate mixture. Pour chocolate mixture into 3-cup freezer tray. Freeze till firm. Break frozen mixture in small pieces with fork. In chilled bowl, beat till smooth. Return to freezer tray. Freeze till firm. Remove from freezer 10 to 15 minutes before serving. Makes 6 servings.

FOUR-FRUIT ICE

Food exchanges/serving: 1 fruit
(Carbohydrate, 10.2 grams; protein, 1.2 grams;
  fat, .1 gram)
44 calories/serving

UNDER 60 CALORIES

Combine 1 large fully ripe banana, mashed; ½ teaspoon grated orange peel; ½ cup orange juice; and 1 tablespoon lemon juice. Beat till smooth. Stir in 1½ cups low-calorie cranberry juice cocktail, noncaloric sweetener to equal ¼ cup sugar, and 5 drops red food coloring. Turn into 4-cup freezer tray; freeze till firm.

Break frozen mixture into chunks in chilled bowl. Using chilled beaters, beat with electric mixer till smooth. Return to tray. Repeat freezing and beating. After second beating, fold in 2 stiffly beaten egg whites. Return to tray. Freeze till firm. Let stand a few minutes before serving. Makes 8 servings.

LIME FREEZE

Food exchanges/serving: ⅓ meat, ¼ fruit
(Carbohydrate, 2.4 grams; protein, 2.8 grams;
  fat, 1.4 grams)
32 calories/serving

UNDER 60 CALORIES

½ cup evaporated skim
  milk
2 egg yolks
  Noncaloric sweetener to
  equal ⅓ cup sugar
½ teaspoon grated lime peel
2 tablespoons lime juice
  Dash salt
3 or 4 drops green food coloring
2 egg whites
2 tablespoons lemon juice

Pour milk into shallow container; freeze till icy cold. Blend egg yolks, sweetener, lime peel, lime juice, salt, and food coloring. Combine milk and egg whites. Beat with electric mixer till fluffy. Add lemon juice; beat to stiff peaks. Beat in egg yolk mixture. Pour into 8½x4½x2⅝-inch loaf pan; freeze till firm. Break into chunks. In chilled bowl beat with electric mixer till smooth. Return to loaf pan; freeze till firm. Makes 8 servings.

CREAMY CHOCOLATE PUDDING

Food exchanges/serving: 1 meat, ¼ fruit
(Carbohydrate, 2.4 grams; protein, 4.2 grams;
fat, 6.4 grams)
80 calories/serving

> 1 **envelope unflavored gelatin**
> 3 **eggs**
> **Noncaloric sweetener to equal**
> **⅓ cup sugar**
> 1 **1-ounce square unsweetened**
> **chocolate, melted and cooled**
> 1 **envelope from a 2½-ounce package**
> **low-calorie dessert topping mix**
> **Shredded orange peel**

Soften gelatin in ¾ cup cold water. Stir over
low heat till gelatin dissolves; cool. Beat eggs
with electric mixer till light and fluffy; beat in
noncaloric sweetener and chocolate. Beat in
gelatin mixture. Prepare topping mix following package directions; fold in chocolate mixture. Chill till mixture mounds. Spoon into 8
dishes. Chill firm. Top with peel. Serves 8.

PINEAPPLE CREME DESSERTS

Food exchanges/serving: ½ fruit, ½ bread, ½ fat
(Carbohydrate, 13.6 grams; protein, 2.0 grams;
fat, 3.3 grams)
89 calories/serving

> 2 **beaten egg yolks**
> 1 **4-serving envelope low-calorie**
> **vanilla pudding mix**
> ½ **cup unsweetened pineapple juice**
> 1 **cup whipped low-calorie dessert**
> **topping**
> 1 **pint fresh strawberries**
> 4 **ladyfingers, halved lengthwise**
> **and crosswise**

Blend yolks and 1½ cups water into pudding
mix. Cook, *stirring constantly*, over low heat
till thickened. Cool, stirring occasionally. Fold
pineapple juice and whipped topping into
pudding. Chill. Divide *half* the pudding among
8 dishes. Reserve 8 berries; halve remaining
berries and spoon into dishes. Top with pudding. Serve with 2 ladyfinger quarters. Top
with reserved berries. Serves 8.

BAKED PUMPKIN PUDDING

Food exchanges/serving: 1 meat, 1 fruit
(Carbohydrate, 11.7 grams; protein, 9.2 grams;
fat, 3.8 grams)
109 calories/serving

Combine 3 beaten eggs, 1 cup canned pumpkin, noncaloric sweetener to equal ⅓ cup
sugar, ½ teaspoon ground cinnamon, ¼ teaspoon ground allspice, and ¼ teaspoon grated
orange peel; slowly stir in one 14½-ounce
can evaporated skim milk. Pour into six 6-
ounce custard cups.

Place in shallow baking pan; pour hot water
around cups to depth of 1 inch. Bake at 325°
till knife inserted off-center comes out clean,
about 60 minutes. Serve warm or chilled.
Garnish with ½ cup *whipped* low-calorie dessert topping and ground cinnamon. Serves 6.

APPLE BREAD PUDDING

Food exchanges/serving: ⅔ meat, 1 fruit, ½ bread
(Carbohydrate, 16.8 grams; protein, 6.0 grams;
fat, 3.2 grams)
114 calories/serving

> 4 **slices white bread**
> 1½ **cups reconstituted nonfat dry milk,**
> **scalded**
> 4 **eggs**
> ½ **teaspoon ground cinnamon**
> ¼ **teaspoon ground nutmeg**
> **Dash salt**
> **Noncaloric sweetener to equal**
> **⅓ cup sugar**
> 1 **medium apple, peeled, cored, and**
> **diced**
> ⅓ **cup raisins**

Toast bread on baking sheet in 350° oven till
golden, about 10 minutes; cut in ½-inch
cubes. Turn into 8¼x1¾-inch round ovenware
dish. Add hot milk; let stand 15 minutes. Beat
together eggs, cinnamon, nutmeg, salt, and
noncaloric sweetener till light. Add apple and
raisins; stir into bread mixture. Place in shallow baking pan; add hot water to larger pan
to depth of ½ inch. Bake at 350° till knife inserted off-center comes out clean, 30 to 35
minutes. Serve warm or chilled. Serves 8.

Just Right for 1 or 2

TWO-FRUIT SLUSH
101 calories/serving

A ruby cranberry slush is topped with fresh apricot slices—

1 cup low-calorie cranberry juice cocktail
4 fresh medium apricots, sliced

Pour cranberry juice cocktail into a freezer tray; freeze just to a slush, 1 to 1½ hours. Break frozen mixture apart with fork, if necessary. Spoon into sherbet dishes; top with apricots. Serve immediately. Makes 2 servings.

TINY LEMON CHEESECAKES
144 calories/serving

Small in size but big in flavor—

1 teaspoon unflavored gelatin
2 tablespoons sugar
¼ cup cold water
⅓ cup dry cottage cheese
⅓ cup yogurt
2 teaspoons lemon juice
¼ teaspoon grated lemon peel
10 drops yellow food coloring
• • •
3 tablespoons nonfat dry milk powder
3 tablespoons icy cold water
1 zwieback, crushed

Combine gelatin and sugar; add cold water. Stir over low heat till gelatin and sugar dissolve. Force cottage cheese through sieve. Add to gelatin mixture along with yogurt, lemon juice, lemon peel, and food coloring; stir. Chill till slightly thickened.

Combine milk powder and icy cold water; beat till soft peaks form. Fold into gelatin mixture. Pour into two 1-cup dishes. Sprinkle with zwieback. Chill till firm. Garnish with lemon peel twists, if desired. Makes 2 servings.

CRANBERRY-GRAPE DESSERTS
97 calories/serving

Two-layered, wine-flavored beauties—

1½ teaspoons unflavored gelatin
1 cup low-calorie cranberry juice cocktail
1 inch stick cinnamon
4 whole cloves
¼ cup seedless green grapes, halved
1 teaspoon unflavored gelatin
1 tablespoon sugar
2 tablespoons dry white wine

Soften 1½ teaspoons gelatin in ¼ *cup* cranberry juice. In saucepan combine remaining cranberry juice, stick cinnamon, and cloves. Heat to boiling; simmer, covered, for 5 minutes. Strain; stir in softened gelatin till dissolved. Chill gelatin mixture till partially set; add *half* the seedless green grapes.

Anchor two 8-ounce glasses in tilted position in 1-quart casserole filled with rock salt or crumpled foil. Pour cranberry gelatin in tilted glasses; chill till firm.

In small saucepan combine 1 teaspoon gelatin and sugar; add ½ cup cold water. Heat and stir till dissolved. Stir in wine; chill till partially set. Fold in remaining grapes. Set glasses of cranberry gelatin upright; pour in wine gelatin. Chill till firm. Makes 2 servings.

APPLE-GRAPEFRUIT COMBO
92 calories/serving

1 small apple, cored and sliced
½ white grapefruit, sectioned
2 tablespoons yogurt
4 teaspoons brown sugar

Combine apple and grapefruit; divide between 2 serving dishes. Stir yogurt and brown sugar together. Spoon yogurt mixture atop each serving. Makes 2 servings.

These Tiny Lemon Cheesecakes, decorated with twists of lemon peel and crushed zwieback, are ideal to prepare if you are a lone dieter. Serve yourself one dessert today and the other one tomorrow.

PETITE GINGER SOUFFLÉS
146 calories/serving

A light and delicate mealtime finale—

- **2 beaten egg yolks**
- **2 tablespoons skim milk**
- **1 tablespoon granulated sugar**
  Dash salt
- **1 teaspoon finely snipped candied ginger**
- **¼ teaspoon vanilla**
- **2 egg whites**
- **¼ teaspoon cream of tartar**
- **1 tablespoon granulated sugar**
- **1 teaspoon powdered sugar**

In small saucepan combine first 4 ingredients. Cook over low heat, stirring constantly, till thickened. Remove from heat; stir in ginger and vanilla. Beat till thick and lemon-colored, about 2 minutes; set aside.

Beat egg whites and cream of tartar to soft peaks. Gradually add 1 tablespoon granulated sugar, beating to stiff peaks. Fold yolk mixture into whites till blended. Spoon into 2 individual soufflé dishes or two 10-ounce baking dishes. Place dishes in shallow baking dish; pour boiling water around dishes to depth of ½ inch. Bake at 350° till tops spring back when lightly touched, 25 to 30 minutes. Sprinkle tops of soufflés with powdered sugar. Serve immediately. Makes 2 servings.

low-calorie desserts
IN MENUS

Wise menu planning during a diet program allows you to have your dessert and eat it, too. The four menus in this section, including this Fruit with Melon Ice menu, illustrate how desserts can satisfy nutritional requirements. The Basic Four Food Groups and the Calorie Chart provide further assistance.

86

<table>
<tr><td>

menu

458 calories

Rolled Rib Roast
Roasted Potato
Grilled Tomato with Cheese
Tossed Green Salad
Fruit with Melon Ice
Coffee

</td><td>

menu

462 calories

Roast Chicken
Broccoli Spears
Sliced Apple-Orange Salad
Chilled Eggnog Soufflé
Skim Milk   Coffee

</td></tr>
</table>

 **FRUIT-VEGETABLE GROUP**

 **MEAT GROUP**

Nutritional Value: Fruits and vegetables are valuable sources of vitamins and minerals, particularly vitamins A and C.

Do not be misled into believing that because fruit is present in a recipe it always satisfies a whole fruit serving. In the menu above, Fruit with Melon Ice (page 8) does contribute one serving per person toward the four servings needed daily. Pineapple Ambrosia Boat (page 53) and Cherry-Rhubarb Pie (page 63), among others would do likewise. But recipes such as Cinnamon-Pear Mold (page 18) and Apricot-Pineapple Kuchen (page 72), with less fruit, count only ½ serving.

Meal Planning: Fruit desserts are favorites of people concerned with weight control. The double features of good nutrition and low-calorie counts make them especially attractive.

Fruits also permit the homemaker to plan variety into any menu. Add texture with Minted Pineapple (page 8), or smoothness with Apricot Spanish Cream (page 58). For something hot, try Cheesy Baked Apples (page 15); or cold, Orange Alaskas (page 32).

Nutritional Value: Foods in the meat group provide protein used by the body for the growth and repair of body tissues, as well as vitamins and minerals such as thiamin, niacin, riboflavin, and iron. Eggs, nuts, and peanut butter are meat group foods that appear as ingredients in dessert recipes. Because of calorie limitations, however, only eggs commonly appear in low-calorie desserts such as custards, puddings, omelets, and soufflés.

Unlike fruits, protein-rich desserts usually can be used to fill only a portion of one meat-serving equivalent. In this menu, for example, the eggs in Chilled Eggnog Soufflé (page 16) fulfill ¼ meat serving requirement. (The milk fulfills part of the milk requirement, too.)

Meal Planning: Protein desserts enable the calorie counter to add lightness and richness at the same time. Baked desserts such as Sweet Strawberry Omelet (page 57), Orange Chiffon Soufflé (page 76), and Petite Ginger Soufflés (page 83) offer a nice temperature contrast to such chilled desserts as Pineapple Sponge (page 29) and Eggnog (page 67).

menu

534 calories

Baked Halibut
Green Beans
Pickled Beets
Dinner Roll   Butter
Baked Caramel Custard
Coffee

menu

488 calories

Broiled Veal Cutlet
Asparagus Spears
Fresh Peach Halves on Lettuce
Bread Pudding
Skim Milk   Coffee

MILK GROUP

BREAD-CEREAL GROUP

Nutritional Value: Milk is the main source of calcium, and also is a good source of protein, riboflavin, vitamin A, vitamin D, and phosphorus. All types of milk—fluid, evaporated, dry, whole, fortified skim, and buttermilk—as well as milk products such as yogurt, cheese, and ice milk are included.

The majority of desserts containing milk provide part of a 1-cup serving equivalent. In the menu example, the Baked Caramel Custard (page 59) is equivalent to ⅓ milk serving. The yogurt in Strawberry-Yogurt Medley (page 73) and the cheese in Pineapple Cheesecake (page 16) add small portions to the day's milk intake, too. Each serving of Spiced Hot Cocoa (page 44) counts as one milk serving.

Meal Planning: Milk desserts serve double duty, since the recipes usually contain ingredients from other food groups. Cheese combines well with fruits as in Baked Apples with Cheese (page 12). In custards and soufflés, milk is teamed with eggs from the meat group. Milk also is common to bread and cereal desserts such as Banana Bread Pudding (page 26).

Nutritional Value: Whole grain, enriched, and restored breads and cereals are rich sources of thiamin, niacin, and riboflavin.

Contrary to popular opinion, breads and cereals can and should be incorporated into low-calorie menus. However, a very limited daily caloric allotment may not always allow you to include all four servings.

Incorporate low-calorie desserts containing breads into menus according to the number of servings you can afford. Bread Pudding (page 29) in the above menu contains only ⅓ bread serving per person; Cherry-Rice Bavarian (page 19), only ¼ serving; and Angel-Lime Dessert (page 22), only ½ serving. Count each serving of cake or the piecrust or crumb crust portion of pie as one bread serving.

Meal Planning: More substantial bread- or cereal-based desserts best complete light meals. For example, Choco-Mint Roll (page 36) and Berry-Rhubarb Shortcake (page 38) are perfect meal cappers for soup-and-salad menus. Plan cookies such as Gingersnaps (page 39) as between-meal refreshments.

Eat the basic 4 foods every day.

MILK GROUP — 2 to 4 cups daily

Includes milk, yogurt, ice cream, and cheese.
  Recommended allowances:
    2 to 3 cups for children
    4 or more cups for teen-agers
    2 or more cups for adults
  Calcium equivalents for 1 cup milk:
    1⅓ ounces Cheddar-type cheese
    1½ cups cottage cheese
    1 pint (2 cups) ice cream

BREAD-CEREAL GROUP — 4 servings daily

Includes whole grain, enriched, or restored
breads, cereals, cornmeal, grits, crackers,
pasta, rice, and quick breads.
  Consider as one serving:
    1 slice bread
    ¾ to 1 cup ready-to-eat cereal
    ½ to ¾ cup cooked cereal, rice, pasta

FRUIT-VEGETABLE GROUP — 4 servings daily

Include one serving of citrus fruit or two servings of tomato daily plus one serving of a dark
green leafy vegetable, deep yellow vegetable,
or yellow fruit 3 to 4 times a week.
  Consider as one serving:
    ½ cup fruit or vegetable
    1 medium apple, banana, or potato
    ½ grapefruit or cantaloupe

MEAT GROUP — 2 servings daily

Includes beef, veal, pork, lamb, poultry, fish,
and eggs. Alternate sources of protein include
dry beans, dry peas, nuts, and peanut butter.
  Consider as one serving:
    2-3 ounces cooked meat, fish, poultry
    2 eggs
    1 cup cooked dry beans or peas
    4 tablespoons peanut butter

Calorie Chart

FOOD	CALORIES
A	
Apple	
Baked, sweetened, 1 medium	188
Brown betty, ½ cup	211
Fresh, 1 medium	70
Juice, canned, 1 cup	120
Applesauce, canned	
Sweetened, ½ cup	115
Unsweetened, ½ cup	50
Apricots	
Canned, ½ cup with syrup	110
Canned, ½ cup with juice	43
Dried, cooked, unsweetened, ½ cup with juice	120
Dried, uncooked, snipped, 1 cup	390
Fresh, 2 to 3 medium	55
Nectar, 1 cup	140
Asparagus	
Canned, spears, green, medium, 6 spears	21
Fresh, cooked, cut spears, ½ cup	15
Avocado, peeled, ½	185
B	
Bacon, 2 crisp strips	90
Bacon, Canadian, 3 slices	195
Baking powder, 1 teaspoon	7
Banana, 1 medium	100
Beans	
Baked with tomato sauce and pork, ½ cup	160
Green, snap, fresh, ½ cup	15
Lima, cooked, ½ cup	130
Red kidney, canned or cooked, ½ cup	115
Beef, cooked	
Corned, canned, 3 ounces	185
Dried, chipped, 2 ounces	115
Hamburger, 3-ounce patty, lean ground beef	185
Hamburger, 3-ounce patty, regular ground beef	245
Liver, fried, 2 ounces	130
Pot roast, lean only, 2½ ounces	140
Rib roast, lean only, 2½ ounces	140
Round steak, 3 ounces	220

FOOD	CALORIES
Beef, cooked, *cont.*	
Sirloin steak, broiled, 3 ounces	330
Tongue, braised, 2 ounces	210
Beets, cooked, diced, ½ cup	27
Biscuit, baking powder, 1 (2½ inch diameter)	140
Blackberries, fresh, ½ cup	43
Blueberries	
Fresh, ½ cup	44
Frozen, unsweetened, 9 ounces	132
Boston cream pie, 1/12 of an 8-inch diameter cake	210
Bouillon cube, 1 cube	5
Bread	
Boston brown, 1 slice (3 x ¾ inch)	100
Corn, 1 piece (2-inch square)	93
French or Vienna, 1 slice	58
Rye, 1 slice	56
White, 1 slice	62
Whole wheat, 1 slice	56
Broccoli, spears, cooked, ½ cup	20
Brussels sprouts, cooked, ½ cup	28
Butter, 1 tablespoon	100
C	
Cabbage	
Cooked, ½ cup	20
Raw, red, shredded, 1 cup	31
Raw, shredded, 1 cup	20
Cake	
Angel, no icing, 1/12 of a 10-inch diameter cake	135
Cupcake, yellow	
Chocolate icing, 1 (2¾-inch diameter)	184
No icing, 1 (2¾-inch diameter)	146
Devil's food	
Chocolate icing, 2 layers, 1/12 of 10-inch diameter cake	593
No icing, 1/12 of 10-inch diameter cake	585
Fruitcake	
Dark, 1 slice (3x3x½ inch)	152
Light, 1 slice (3x3x½ inch)	156
Gingerbread, 2x2x2 inches	175
Pound, 1 slice (3x3x½ inch)	142

FOOD	CALORIES
Cake, *cont.*	
Sponge, no icing, 1/12 of a 10-inch diameter cake	195
Yellow	
Chocolate icing, 2 layer, 1/12 of 9-inch diameter cake	366
No icing, 1/12 of 9-inch diameter cake	263
Candy	
Caramels, 1 ounce (3 medium)	115
Chocolate creams, 1 ounce (2 to 3 pieces)	125
Chocolate, milk, 1-ounce bar	150
Chocolate mints, 1 ounce (1 to 2 mints)	115
Gumdrops, 1 ounce (2½ large or 20 small)	100
Jelly beans, 10 beans	105
Peanut brittle, 1 piece (2½x1¼x⅜ inch)	120
Cantaloupe, ¼ (5-inch diameter)	30
Carrots	
Cooked, diced, ½ cup	20
Raw, 1 large or 2 small	42
Catsup, 1 tablespoon	18
Cauliflower	
Cooked, flowerets, ½ cup	10
Raw, flowerets, 1 cup	27
Celery, raw, two 8-inch stalks	10
Cereal, cooked	
Cream of wheat, regular, ¾ cup	99
Oatmeal, ¾ cup	100
Cereal, ready-to-eat	
Bran flakes, ¾ cup	100
Cornflakes, ¾ cup	72
Oats, puffed, ¾ cup	78
Rice, puffed, ¾ cup	39
Wheat, flakes, ¾ cup	93
Cheese	
American, process, 1 ounce	107
Blue, 1 ounce	105
Cheddar, 1 ounce	115
Cottage, cream-style, from skim milk, 1 cup	239
Cottage, dry, 1 cup	192
Cream cheese, 1 ounce	106
Neufchâtel, 1 ounce	73
Parmesan, grated, 3 tablespoons	60
Soufflé, home recipe, 3½ ounces	218

FOOD	CALORIES

Cheese, *cont.*
Spread, American, 1 ounce ... 81
Swiss, 1 ounce 105
Cherries
Canned, tart or sweet, ½ cup
with syrup 89
Canned, tart or sweet, red,
½ cup with water 53
Fresh, sweet, ½ cup 40
Chicken
A la king, cooked,
3½ ounces 191
Chow mein, 3½ ounces 102
Fried, bone removed
Dark meat, skinned,
3½ ounces 220
Light meat, skinned,
3½ ounces 197
Potpie, 1 individual
(4½-inch diameter) 535
Roasted, bone removed
Dark meat, skinned,
3½ ounces 176
Light meat, skinned,
3½ ounces 166
Chili con carne with beans,
canned, ½ cup 167
Chili sauce, 1 tablespoon 17
Chocolate
Semisweet pieces, 1 cup 860
Sweet, plain, 1 ounce 133
Syrup, thin-type, canned,
1 tablespoon 50
Unsweetened, 1 ounce 145
Chop suey, with meat,
3½ ounces 120
Clam
Canned, ½ cup in liquor 52
Chowder
Manhattan, 1 serving 153
New England, 1 serving 259
Cocoa, whole milk, 1 cup 235
Cocoa powder, unsweetened,
1 tablespoon 21
Coconut, shredded, dried
2 tablespoons 83
Coffee, 1 cup 5
Cola, carbonated beverage,
1 cup 95
Coleslaw, no lettuce, ⅔ cup 68
Cookie
Brownie, unfrosted, 1 95
Butter, thin
(2½-inch diameter) 50
Chocolate chip, 1 50
Chocolate wafer, 1 37
Fig bar, 1 50
Gingersnap, 1 28
Macaroon, 1 85
Sugar (3-inch diameter) 89
Vanilla wafer, 3 51

FOOD	CALORIES

Corn
Canned, whole kernel,
½ cup 85
Fresh, cooked, 1 ear
(5x1¾ inches) 70
Cornstarch, 1 tablespoon 29
Corn syrup, 1 tablespoon 60
Crab
Imperial, 1 serving 235
Meat, canned, flaked, ½ cup . 85
Crackers
Cheese, round, 1 17
Graham, 1 (2½-inch square) . . 28
Rusk, 1 piece 50
Saltine, 2 (2-inch square) 35
Soda, 2 (2½-inch square) 50
Cranberries
Fresh, 1 cup 46
Juice cocktail
Canned, 1 cup 165
Low-cal, 1 cup 60
Sauce, sweetened,
canned, 1 cup 405
Cream
Half-and-half, 1 tablespoon . . . 20
Heavy or whipping,
1 tablespoon 55
Light, 1 tablespoon 30
Whipped, unsweetened,
1 tablespoon 28
Cucumber, 6 slices (2x⅛ inch) . . 5
Custard, baked, whole milk,
½ cup 152

D-F

Dates, fresh and dried, pitted,
1 cup 490
Doughnut
Cake-type, plain, 1 125
Sugar, with icing, 1 151
Yeast-type, plain, 1 124
With jelly center, 1 226
Egg
Fried, 1 large 100
Omelet, plain, 1 large egg 110
Poached, hard- or
soft-cooked, 1 large 78
Scrambled with milk and
butter, 1 egg 110
White only, medium, 1 15
Whole, large, 1 88
Whole, medium, 1 80
Yolk only, medium, 1 60
Eggplant, cooked, drained,
diced, ½ cup 19
Endive, raw, 20 long leaves 20
Figs
Canned, ½ cup with syrup . . . 110
Dried, 1 large 60
Fresh, 3 small 90

FOOD	CALORIES

Fish
Bass, baked, 3 ounces 216
Haddock, fried, 3 ounces 144
Halibut, broiled,
3 ounces 155
Ocean perch, fried, 3 ounces 195
Salmon
Broiled or baked,
3 ounces 154
Canned, pink, ½ cup 188
Canned, red, ½ cup 215
Loaf, 1 serving 122
Tuna
Canned in oil, drained,
½ cup 160
Canned in water, ½ cup . . . 144
Casserole with noodles,
1 serving 280
Salad, 1 serving 170
Fish stick, breaded, 1 40
Flour
Cake, sifted, 1 cup 364
Wheat, all-purpose,
enriched, sifted, 1 cup 400
Wheat, all-purpose,
enriched, 1 tablespoon 25
Frankfurter, cooked, 1 140
Frosting
Chocolate, 1 cup 1,035
White, boiled, 1 cup 300
Fruit cocktail, canned, ½ cup
with syrup 100

G

Gelatin dessert
Fruit added, prepared,
½ cup 80
Plain, prepared, ½ cup 70
Low-cal, ½ cup 8
Gelatin, dry, unflavored,
1 tablespoon 34
Ginger ale, 1 cup 80
Ginger, candied, 1 ounce 92
Gooseberries, fresh ⅔ cup 39
Grapefruit
Canned, segments, white,
½ cup with syrup 90
Canned, segments, ½ cup
with juice 45
Fresh
Pink, ½ medium 50
White, ½ medium 45
Juice
Canned, sweetened,
1 cup 130
Canned, unsweetened,
1 cup 100
Fresh, 1 cup 95
Frozen, reconstituted,
1 cup 100

FOOD	CALORIES	FOOD	CALORIES	FOOD	CALORIES

Grapes
 Concord, fresh, ½ cup....... 33
 Green, fresh, ½ cup........ 48
 Juice
  Canned, 1 cup...........165
  Frozen, reconstituted,
  1 cup 135
Gravy, beef, home recipe,
 ¼ cup.................... 60

H-M

Ham, fully cooked,
 3½ ounces.................219
Hard sauce, 2 tablespoons 97
Honey, 1 tablespoon 65
Honeydew melon, ¼ small
 (5-inch diameter) 33
Ice cream, vanilla, 10% fat,
 ½ cup.....................128
Ice milk, ½ cup 100
Jam, 1 tablespoon............ 55
 Low-cal, 1 tablespoon 21
Jelly, 1 tablespoon 50
 Low-cal, 1 tablespoon....... 21
Ladyfinger, 1 large 50
Lamb, cooked
 Loin chop, 3½ ounces.......223
 Rib chop, 3½ ounces 291
 Roast leg, whole,
 3½ ounces...............195
Lard, 1 tablespoon 126
Lemon
 Fresh, 1 medium............ 20
 Juice, 1 tablespoon.......... 4
Lemonade, frozen,
 reconstituted, 1 cup 110
Lettuce, iceberg, ¼ medium
 compact head.............. 15
Lime
 Fresh, 1 medium............ 28
 Juice, 1 tablespoon.......... 4
Limeade, frozen, reconstituted,
 1 cup 100
Lobster
 Canned, ½ cup............. 75
 Thermidor, 1 lobster in shell 405
Luncheon meat
 Bologna, 1 thin slice
 (4-inch diameter) 86
 Ham, boiled, 1 ounce 68
 Salami, 1 slice (3¾-inch
 diameter, ¼ inch thick).... 130
Macaroni, cooked, ½ cup...... 78
Macaroni and cheese, baked,
 ½ cup.....................235
Malted milk, 1 cup............280
Mandarin oranges, 3½ ounces
 with syrup 60
Maple syrup, 1 tablespoon 50
Maraschino cherry, 1 10

Margarine, 1 tablespoon 100
Marmalade, orange,
 1 tablespoon 56
Marshmallow, 1 25
Meat loaf, beef and pork,
 1 slice (4x3x⅝ inches) 264
Melba toast, 1 thin slice 15
Milk
 Buttermilk, 1 cup 90
 Chocolate drink, 1 cup......190
 Condensed, sweetened,
 undiluted, ½ cup 490
 Dried, nonfat, instant,
 1 cup 246
 Evaporated, skim, undiluted,
 ½ cup................... 86
 Evaporated, whole undiluted,
 ½ cup...................172
 Skim, 1 cup............... 82
 Skim, fortified, 1 cup.......105
 Skim, 2% fat, 1 cup.......145
 Whole, 1 cup 160
Molasses, light, 1 tablespoon ... 50
Muffin
 Blueberry, 1 average.........112
 Corn, 1 (2¾-inch diameter) .. 150
 Plain, 1 (2¾-inch diameter) .. 140
Mushrooms
 Canned, solids and liquid,
 ½ cup................... 17
 Fresh, 10 small or 4 large 28
Mussels, 3½ ounces........... 95
Mustard, prepared,
 1 tablespoon 12

N-O

Nectarines, fresh, 2 medium ... 64
Noodles, cooked, ½ cup.......100
Nuts
 Almonds, dried, salted,
 unblanched, 13 to 15......105
 Brazil nuts, 4............... 97
 Cashews, roasted, 4 to 5..... 95
 Peanuts, roasted, shelled,
 chopped, 1 tablespoon 55
 Pecans, chopped,
 1 tablespoon............. 50
 Walnuts, chopped,
 1 tablespoon 50
Okra, cooked, 8 pods
 (3 x ⅝ inch) 25
Olives, green, 4 medium....... 15
Olives, ripe, 3 small........... 15
Onion
 Cooked, ½ cup............. 30
 Green, 6 small without tops.. 20
 Mature, raw, chopped,
 1 tablespoon............. 5
Orange
 Navel, 1 medium 73

Orange, *cont.*
 Juice
  Canned, unsweetened,
  1 cup 120
  Fresh, 1 cup.............115
  Frozen, reconstituted,
  1 cup 120
Oysters
 Raw, ½ cup
 (6 to 10 medium) 80
 Stew, 1 cup (3 to 4 oysters)... 200

P

Pancake (4-inch diameter)
 Buckwheat, 1 55
 Plain, 1 60
Papaya, 1 medium 120
Parsnips, cooked, ½ cup....... 50
Peaches
 Canned, 2 medium halves
 with 2 tablespoons syrup .. 90
 Canned, sliced, ½ cup with
 juice 43
 Dried, uncooked, 1 cup.....420
 Fresh, 1 medium........... 35
 Frozen, sweetened, ½ cup ... 105
Peanut butter, 1 tablespoon..... 95
Pears
 Canned, 2 medium halves
 and 2 tablespoons syrup ... 90
 Canned, ½ cup with juice ... 60
 Canned, ½ cup with water... 36
 Fresh, 1 medium...........100
Peas, green, cooked, ½ cup.... 58
Pepper, green, raw, 1 medium .. 10
Pickle relish
 Sour, 3½ ounces............ 19
 Sweet, 3½ ounces 138
Pickles
 Dill, 1 large............... 15
 Sweet, 1 medium 30
Pie, ⅙ of a 9-inch pie
 Apple 410
 Butterscotch...............408
 Cherry 410
 Custard...................333
 Lemon meringue...........357
 Mince....................426
 Pecan....................571
 Pumpkin..................317
Pineapple
 Canned, ½ cup with syrup ... 98
 Canned, ½ cup with juice ... 72
 Fresh, diced, ½ cup......... 38
 Juice
  Canned, unsweetened,
  1 cup 135
  Frozen, reconstituted,
  1 cup 102
Pizza, cheese, ⅛ of 14-inch pie 185

FOOD	CALORIES
Plums	
Canned, ½ cup with syrup	100
Canned, ½ cup with juice	78
Fresh, 1 (2-inch diameter)	25
Pomegranate, fresh, 1 medium	63
Popcorn	
Plain, 1 cup	25
With oil and salt, 1 cup	40
Pork, cooked	
Chop, loin center cut, lean only, 3½ ounces	250
Sausage, cooked, links or patty, 3½ ounces	421
Tenderloin, 3½ ounces	239
Potatoes	
Baked, 1 medium	90
Boiled, 1 medium	80
Chips, 10 medium	115
French-fried, 10 medium	155
Hashed brown, ½ cup	225
Mashed with milk, ½ cup	63
Salad, ½ cup	99
Sweet	
Baked, 1 medium	155
Candied, 1 medium	295
Canned, ½ cup	118
Pretzels, 5 regular sticks	10
Prune juice, canned, 1 cup	200
Prunes, dried, cooked, unsweetened, ½ cup	148
Pudding, cornstarch	
Butterscotch, ½ cup	207
Chocolate, ½ cup	219
Tapioca, ½ cup	110
Vanilla, ½ cup	152
Pumpkin	
Canned, 1 cup	75
Seeds, 3½ ounces	553

R

FOOD	CALORIES
Radishes, raw, 4 small	5
Raisins, 1 cup	480
Raspberries	
Black, fresh, ½ cup	50
Red, fresh, ½ cup	35
Red, frozen, sweetened, ½ cup	120
Rhubarb	
Cooked, sweetened, ½ cup	193
Fresh, ¾ to 1 cup	16
Rice	
Brown, cooked, ½ cup	88
White, cooked, ½ cup	113
Roll	
Hamburger, 1 medium	89
Hard, 1 medium	109
Plain, 1 medium	113
Sweet, 1 medium	178
Romaine, raw, 3½ ounces	18
Rutabaga, cooked, ½ cup	35

S

FOOD	CALORIES
Salad dressing	
Blue cheese, 1 tablespoon	71
Low-cal, 1 tablespoon	11
French, 1 tablespoon	57
Low-cal, 1 tablespoon	13
Italian, 1 tablespoon	77
Low-cal, 1 tablespoon	6
Mayonnaise, 1 tablespoon	101
Mayonnaise-type, 1 tablespoon	61
Low-cal, 1 tablespoon	19
Thousand Island, 1 tablespoon	70
Low-cal, 1 tablespoon	25
Salad oil, 1 tablespoon	125
Sandwich, 1 slice white bread	
Bacon, lettuce, tomato	282
Chicken salad	245
Egg salad	279
Ham	281
Peanut butter	328
Roast beef, hot, with 3 tablespoons gravy	429
Roast pork, hot, with 3 tablespoons gravy	503
Tuna salad	278
Sauerkraut, canned, ½ cup	20
Scallops, cooked, 3½ ounces	112
Sherbet, ½ cup	130
Shortening, all-purpose, 1 tablespoon	125
Shrimp	
Canned, 3 ounces	100
French-fried, 3 ounces	191
Soup, condensed, diluted with water unless specified otherwise	
Beef bouillon, broth, consommé, 1 cup	30
Chicken noodle, 1 cup	65
Cream of celery, diluted with milk, 1 cup	166
Cream of mushroom, diluted with milk, 1 cup	211
Split-pea, 1 cup	145
Tomato, diluted with milk, 1 cup	169
Vegetable with beef broth, 1 cup	80
Sour cream, ½ cup	242
Low-cal, imitation, ½ cup	144
Spaghetti, cooked, ½ cup	83
Spaghetti with meatballs in tomato sauce, home recipe, 1 cup	335
Spanish rice, 1 cup	130
Spinach	
Frozen, chopped, cooked, ½ cup	23

FOOD	CALORIES
Squash	
Summer, cooked, diced, ½ cup	15
Winter, baked, mashed, ½ cup	65
Strawberries	
Fresh, ½ cup	28
Frozen, sweetened, ½ cup	140
Sugar	
Brown, packed, 1 tablespoon	50
Brown, packed, 1 cup	820
Granulated, 1 tablespoon	46
Granulated, 1 cup	770
Powdered, 1 tablespoon	29
Powdered, 1 cup	460

T-Z

FOOD	CALORIES
Tangerine	
Fresh, 1 medium	40
Juice, canned, 1 cup	125
Tapioca, granulated, 1 tablespoon	36
Tartar sauce, 1 tablespoon	95
Tea, 1 cup	2
Tomato	
Canned, ½ cup	25
Fresh, 1 medium	35
Juice, canned, 1 cup	40
Paste, canned, 3½ ounces	82
Turkey, roasted, 3 slices (3x2½x¼ inches)	200
Turnip, cooked, diced, ½ cup	20
Veal, cooked	
Cutlet, 3½ ounces	202
Loin chop, 3½ ounces	207
Sirloin roast, 3½ ounces	176
Vegetable juice cocktail, 1 cup	40
Vinegar, 1 tablespoon	2
Waffle, 1 (5½x4½x½ inches)	210
Water chestnuts, 4	20
Watercress, raw, 3½ ounces	19
Watermelon, 4x8-inch wedge	115
Welsh rarebit, 3½ ounces	179
Whipped topping	
Frozen, 1 tablespoon	16
Powdered, whipped, 1 tablespoon	14
Low-cal, 1 tablespoon	7
White sauce, medium, ½ cup	215
Wine	
Dessert, 3½ ounces	140
Table (dry), 3½ ounces	85
Yeast, active dry, 1 package	20
Yogurt	
Fruit-flavored, ½ cup	135
Plain, made from skim milk, ½ cup	63
Plain, made from whole milk, ½ cup	75
Zwieback, 1 piece	31

Index

Acknowledgement: Many of the calorie counts for charts and recipes in this book were determined by using information from *Composition of Foods,* by Bernice K. Watt and Annabel L. Merrill (Washington, D.C., Agriculture Handbook Number 8, United States Department of Agriculture, 1963); from *Nutritive Value of Foods* (Washington, D.C., Home and Garden Bulletin No. 72, United States Department of Agriculture, 1970); and from *Food Values of Portions Commonly Used,* by Anna de Planter Bowes and Charles F. Church (Tenth Edition, Philadelphia, J. P. Lippincott Co., 1966).